An Enlisted Man's Point of View: Lessons Learned in the 199th 1966-1967

Lee H. Houston

An Enlisted Man's Point of View:
Lesson Learned in the 199th 1966-1967

Copyrighted 2020
By Lee H. Houston, Jr.

ISBN 978-0-578-68742-1

Published by Dunn & Houston
Carroll County, Virginia, U.S.A.
2020
Mailing address:
2582 Fries Road
Galax, VA 24333

Table of Contents

About the Author

Lee Houston is a former businessperson and educator turned Methodist Pastor. After serving in the United States Army in Vietnam, a Purple Heart recipient, he graduated from North Carolina State University with a BS in Industrial Engineering and started his business career working his way up the corporate ladder to be president of three companies. In the middle of his business career, he left business and returned to education earning a Masters in Communication from the University of North Carolina at Greensboro, served on the staff at North Carolina State University, and taught at two smaller colleges. He also served on several boards and ran his own consulting business. He has had numerous articles published in trade magazines, had a monthly column in one, published two religious books, and spoke many times to trade organizations. All of this has taken him to twenty-six countries. Today, he enjoys serving three small churches full of beautiful people.

Preface

If you are interested in infantry combat, this book may appeal to you. I tell this story from my point of view as an enlisted man in one of the most successful combat operations in the Vietnam War, Operation Fairfax. It is an overlooked point of view, for our part of the war was often close and personal. I am testifying as one of the soldiers who did the fighting and the killing. It has been more than fifty years since I was a machine gunner in the 199th Light Infantry Brigade in Vietnam. Consequently, I do not remember many of the names of the men with whom I fought nor the precise places we did battle nor the exact sequence of events. Some of my memories are a bit sketchy, particularly the more painful ones. However, I have done my best to be as close to the truth as my recollections will permit.

This book does more than what the title says; using the language of GIs, it exposes the thinking of the time. It takes the reader on a brief journey over an exciting decade: from the end of segregation to the start of integration; from Search and Destroy missions to the era of protest and changing values; from a male-dominated world to the beginning of a gender-neutral society, it's in this book.

I also write about learning to live with many violent combat experiences that contribute to my Post Traumatic Stress Disorder (PTSD). Trying to pick the encounters that caused my problems is kind of like sprinting through a great briar patch and then looking back to see which briars cut me. Many of the cuts are still bleeding, for I relive them almost every night. That is the reason for this book. For decades, I avoided even mentioning that I am a Vietnam veteran and had no desire for friendships with my Vietnam comrades. I lived the life of a success-driven workaholic. This book was to identify painful recollections. I found that writing them down in an organized fashion took these memories out of my dreams and put them into my past where they belonged.

This book is a tribute to these fine people at the Veterans Administration. I particularly thank my psychiatrist, Doctor David Dalrymple, and my social worker, Geralyn Conway, LCSW, who have brought me along this far. I also thank Robyn Grage for offering great suggestions for improvements, designing the cover, and doing the book layout. I thank Doctor J. Sanders Huguenin, Associate Professor of History at the University of Virginia at Wise, for reviewing the book and making valuable recommendations. I thank Courtenay Houston for proofreading the final draft. These people all gave unselfishly of their time to help this novice writer express tell not only my story, but also a story too many old soldiers carry yet unexpressed

I dedicate this book to

Judy Dunn Houston,

my wife of fifty years,
thanking her for the many
times she has had her sleep
disturbed by this old GI's
nightmares.

Chapter 1: Your are in the Army Now

It was the time of a military draft. This draft provided soldiers, sailors, and airmen for our armed forces, particularly for our war in Vietnam. By 1970, your birth date was your lottery number, your chance to miss the draft. According to our National Archives, approximately 27 million American men were eligible for military service between 1964 and 1973. The draft raised 2,215,000 men who served in the United States, Southeast Asia, West Germany, and other stations. At the same time, local draft boards granted deferments to 15,400,000 young men. Deferments could be granted for mental or physical reasons, family hardships, and even because one was a student in college. Some of those who served felt cheated because 209,517 men illegally resisted the draft while another 100,000 deserted from our armed forces. Of those deserters, more than 30,000 immigrated to Canada. If you wore the uniform, you share these memories, and went through something like I am about to describe.

I grew up in a small town in the middle of North Carolina's Uwharrie National Forest. The forest's edge was within a hundred yards of our home. My friends and I lived and played in that Forest. An extension of that play was being a Boy Scout. *Boys Life*, the Boy Scouting magazine, regularly featured articles about how to make useful camping gear such as pots and pans out of mothers' empty food cans, how to fold blankets to make a sleeping bag, and how to build shelters from tree branches and leaves. We did it all. We could read maps, use a compass to go from point A to point B, and were proficient in first aid. We knew how to be quiet in the woods and how to shoot. We had single-shot bolt-action 22-caliber rifles. We shot 22 shorts because they were the quietest rounds and did not frighten squirrels and rabbits away.

My family molded me. Dad did more than encourage me to work; from age 14 on, a summer job of some sort was mandatory. He was a hard worker whose favorite saying was, "You can be anything you want to be." Mom also had a basic rule, "I expect you to be a gentleman." She demanded that no matter the circumstances. Born in 1879, my Grandfather Warren, who grew up under difficult circumstances, had a favorite motto, "You have to play the hand you are dealt." They all expected me to be a leader. I was a leader starting in Boy Scouts and on into high school being vice president of my senior high school class and co-captain of the football team. My grades were above average, but certainly not without blemish.

From high school, it was off to Raleigh and North Carolina State College. Dad told me that he would pay my tuition, buy my books, and give me an allowance until I graduated college, married, or joined the service. With all of that going for me, why did I enlist in the Army?

My American heritage goes back to 1631. Most every generation from then until now had some ancestor serve in our military. My Dad enlisted in June of 1939 and served until WORLD WAR II ended. He stayed in the National Guard while he went to college on the GI Bill. The Korean War saw him called back. When the Vietnam War started heating up, duty began to call me. Besides, I needed to "grow-up," for I was not applying myself in college. Therefore, in 1965, after nearly three and a half years in college, during the Thanksgiving holidays I went to see an army recruiter carrying with me a letter from our ROTC commanding officer, a major. The letter attested to my having completed two years of ROTC at North Carolina State University. The major said that my ROTC experience would start me off with E-2 pay.

The recruiter gave me the tests. At a later meeting, he told me which schools I qualified for based on my test results. I listened. He then asked, "Do any of these appeal to you?" I said, "No, I want to go into the airborne infantry. I want to fight." He then went back to telling about the Military Occupational Specialties (MOS) that could lead to good jobs when I got out of the service. "No, I want to go into the combat arm; I want to go into the infantry." He began to tell me about more schools. "How about any of these?" "No, I want to go into the airborne infantry." "Okay, you dumb SOB, I'll sign you up for the airborne infantry. That requires a three-year enlistment." I told him that I wanted to finish the semester; it ended in January. When I finished my enlistment, I wanted to go back to school immediately. That is what he set up.

We had a few days' break after final exams, so it was home for a last few days with my friends and family before reporting for service. The recruiter had told me to wear worn-out clothes, carry only a small tube of toothpaste, a toothbrush, my billfold with driver's license, and $20. The night my friends went back to college, I rode with them and slept in a friend's dorm room on a mattress and pillow but with no sheets or pillowcase. The next morning, it was a two-mile walk to downtown Raleigh and the enlistment depot.

The sun was yet to rise as I joined a rather large group of young men and entered the depot. Only a few of us were volunteers; the Army was considering most of the men for the draft. Many were openly expressing hopes of failing the Army's tests and physical exams. The sergeant in charge segregated volunteers to one side of the room next to a cold wall and a large loading-dock-sized door. It was a poor place to take tests, for lighting was scant, the wall cold, and the door drafty. After hours of testing, they moved us to an adjoining room for our physical exams. There, we went from one station to the next answering medical questions. Medics weighed us, measured us, took our blood pressure and so forth. Then a medic told us to disrobe. Standing naked along with what I would guess was well over a hundred men was an embarrassing experience. Then in walked a captain, a medical officer, who said words to the effect, "You men, keep your mouth shut unless I tell you to open it." Then he checked our prostate glands and checked for ruptures. Not only was that uncomfortable, that room was so cold many turned blue.

We dressed and waited in the test room for what seemed hours. Finally, the sergeant in charge began to call names, having some go to the right of the room and others to the left. What we did not know was that he was separating those the Army would accept from those who failed. The number of men on my side of the room was one half as large as the number on the other side; at that time, the Army was turning down more than two-thirds of those told to report for the draft. That would change as the Vietnam War heated up.

Finally, as darkness began outside, a specialist conducted those selected to another room where a smiling second lieutenant spoke for a minute, then asked us to raise our right hand and repeat after him. Even though my DD-214 says I joined in February, he gave us the oath to defend our country in January of 1966. He congratulated us as having become members of the finest military in the world. He then turned us over to a corporal, a man of few words who spoke a commanding voice, "Follow me."

The corporal led us to a nearby hotel. There, he assigned us rooms, put one man in each room in charge, and gave that man the room key along with our meal tickets. He then said to the men in charge, "Have your men fed, here in this lobby and ready to go at 0600."

We had all grown up in a segregated society and gone to segregated schools. Here we were, black and white, eating supper together. Other

people in the restaurant let us know that they
disapproved with their frowns. One of us, Oliver,
drafted because he was a mortician, was from
Raleigh. Oliver was black. He was the last new
acquaintance we would make who we called by his
first name, for beginning the next day, we referred to
each other only by our rank and last name.

Oliver announced that he knew a great
nightspot not far from the hotel. Most were
frightened to leave the hotel, but eight or ten of us
looked forward to a little excitement and said, "Let's
go." Oliver led us to "The Cave," an all-black
nightclub. Socializing together was a new
experience for both blacks and whites; right up front
our host assured us that since we were now in the
Army, there would be no trouble. Still, some of the
other patrons looked somewhat amazed. However,
the waitress was accommodating. It was a
weeknight, so the place was far from full. We
talked, laughed, and sang along with the jukebox
while listening to James Brown, Sam Cook, The
Temptations, who sang *My Girl*, and the like. After
a few hours, we decided to go back to the hotel, get
some sleep, and ready ourselves for our first full day
in the Army. As we walked back, some of my old
classmates rode by. They did not see me, but I felt a
little choke in my throat.

At 0600, the corporal called the roll; we were
all there. He then walked us back to the depot
where three commercial buses waited. We filled
one bus and then the next as the corporal called our
names: Allen, Blackstock, on down to Zerbach.

Dawn came about the time we left Raleigh. It was cold with a clear, deep blue sky. As we traveled down the highway, there was little conversation on the bus. Many slept. We had no idea where we were going until we rolled through the front gate of Fort Jackson, South Carolina.

A corporal unloaded us in alphabetical order directing each man to his set of yellow footprints painted on the road. We were in formation in front of a WORLD WAR II-era building. The corporal had us turn to our left and walk single file to a large warehouse. There we moved from one station to the next. At the first station, a soldier measured us; another wrote down our dimensions on a paper and placed it in our left hand. At the next station, we received a duffel bag. That soldier showed us exactly how to hold the duffel bag alongside that paper. We now moved and waited, moved and waited. At each of the next stations, a soldier looked at our size and put some part of our uniforms in the duffel bag: 4 fatigue trousers, 4 pairs of socks, 4 sets of boxer shorts, 4 tee-shirts, 1 hat, 1 belt, 2 pair of boots, 1 field jacket, 1 overcoat, 2 towels, and 2 wash clothes. Someone gave us a "Gift Box." It contained a complimentary toothbrush, toothpaste, soap, and razors. Lastly, in the duffel bag went 4 fatigue shirts with our surnames printed over our right pocket and US ARMY over the left. The Army had issued us everything we would need in basic training. We disrobed. Put on our uniforms and did something, I do not remember what, with our civilian clothes.

Whatever it was, we did not see them again. Our uniforms made us equal.

While our clothes fit, we looked sloppy. We all had grown up wearing tight blue jeans low on our hips held up by a narrow belt. The jeans were a bit too short so all could see our white socks and we wore sport shirts with the sleeves rolled up. One man complained that his new pants did not fit. A corporal loudly informed him that women wore pants and men wore trousers. Further, he said the proper place for trousers was around one's waist and not on one's hips like some civilian slob. Most did not know that, nor how to properly tuck our shirts nor blouse our boots nor what a gig line was. A number of men had never even had on a pair of boots.

From there it was to our barracks where we found nothing remotely glamorous. Things were basic and very clean. We were in a world where privacy did not exist; we slept in one large room on bunk beds; neither the toilets or showers had stalls. We simply had to get over the embarrassment of having a grunting stinking bowel movement in front of other men. Another corporal showed us how to make our beds, hang a towel and a washcloth at our bunk's end. The corporal explained that our barracks were to be spotless; he ensured us that enforcement of sanitation would be severe. There were no footlockers; we were to live out of our duffel bags for the next few days. Now, it was back outside.

The corporal explained the boundaries of our area and threatened to have any individual who left that zone charged with desertion. The area was roughly half the size of a football field. Army buildings normally have a three- or four-inch-high number painted on the corner of every building; not here. Every building in the area had a single large number painted on every side. There was this loud public address system easily heard throughout the area; every few minutes someone would announce words to the effect, "Private Johnson, go to the building with three painted on it. That is one, two, three – three Private Johnson. Private Johnson, go in building three through the door next to the road." For the few days, we moved slowly from one numbered building to the next to stand at something resembling parade rest until called. We took more tests, more physicals, and shots immunizing us from what diseases we knew not. We were processing in.

When we were not waiting in lines, the army began teaching us the most basic military skills like how to police our area by picking up cigarette butts and even the smallest piece of trash. This was when cigarettes cost a quarter a pack and many smoked. Smokers quickly learned to tear cigarette butts into tiny parts and then roll those parts into balls the size of grains of sand before discarding them. The Army called that "field stripping." In our area, all paths were marked on each side by a line of rocks. Some of us had to paint these rocks white. We learned to eat in less than five minutes. Each night, a sergeant would come and post a number of us as guards around the perimeter of our area or around some of the buildings nearby. These "hurry up and wait" lines and small jobs kept us busy for three days; then, more buses arrived to take us to basic training. Again, we had no idea where that was.

After several hours, we went through the gate of Fort Gordon, Georgia. Here Drill Instructors (DIs) unloaded us rapidly from the buses. Again, we stood on yellow footprints that arranged us into three platoons each with a DI standing in front. The DIs had us place our duffel bags to our right. Our leaders had gone from being corporals to being sergeants. The DI of our platoon introduced himself as Staff Sergeant Stulls. He stood perfectly erect. He was lean, of medium build, and stood 5 feet 10 inches tall. His uniform was flawless with a tailored blouse tucked with no bulging above his DIs' belt. Below were perfectly fitting trousers. His blouse and trousers were sharply creased. On his head squarely sat a campaign hat with brim absolutely flat and parallel with the ground. On his feet were spit-shined boots. His appearance told us, this is a soldier. He asked in a commanding voice, "Anyone with prior military experience or ROTC training stand forward." I stepped forward. He made me a platoon guide and four others who had some sort of military training he appointed squad leaders. Sergeant Stulls had us move away from our duffel bags. He then had me show the men how to dress-right-dress and basic marching moves. After an hour or two, he seemed satisfied and had us pick up our duffel bags and marched us into our barracks.

He had us make our beds and then checked each bed, demanding better jobs. Then, it was how to arrange our clothes in our footlockers and so forth. A loud whistle blew, and Sergeant Stulls said that whistle blowing was the signal to assemble the company.

We ran out of the barracks and into our first company formation where we met the senior drill instructor. I do not remember his name. He explained that when he, or any other sergeant, spoke to us that we would answer his question starting with the word "Sergeant." He then used colorful, expletive-laced language, I will be a bit milder, to say words to the effect, "I do not care whether you are a damn red man, or a yellow bastard, or a black SOB, or poor white trash. I do not care whether you are Roman Catholic, Protestant, or even a dumb-ass atheist; I do not care whether you are a hick from hot, ugly Georgia or a gang member from that nasty, stinking New York City – in this man's Army, you are all green. Do you hear me?" After a little prodding, we all answered loudly, "Sergeant, yes, Sergeant." He then got within an inch of one poor man's nose and asked what race he was, and the man answered, "Sergeant, I am white." The senior DI screamed, "You are a dumb ass!" Still inches from the man's face, he asked us, "Men, what color is this dumb ass?" We all answered, "Sergeant, that dumb ass is green." "I can't hear you! What color is this dumb ass?" After more prodding, we all screamed, "Sergeant, that dumb ass is green!" It did not take too many days to realize that "dumb ass!" was the senior DI's core expression.

The next few weeks were busy. Our DIs taught us basic military skills and discipline. As for the skills, except for the gas training and firing the M-14, I had become proficient in them in Boy Scouts or in ROTC, but I did not see E-2 pay until everyone else did. One thing we did learn was how to eat faster. I had grown up with two brothers, a sister, and twenty-eight aunts and uncles that had provided me with many cousins. I had to eat fast if I expected to get my growing boy's fill. That speed of eating was nothing compared with what Basic Training required. We started eating as the cooks were putting food on our trays, as we walked to our tables and gobbled down our food until some sergeant would shout, "Move out ladies!" Into our pockets went any fruits such as apples or maybe a biscuit, for the sergeant inspected our trays. They had to be clean of food before we dumped our trash and put the trays, cups, and utensils onto a counter for some poor KP to wash. I did not understand the reason for forcing us to eat fast until I was in Vietnam and sometimes had to eat C-Rations while I slogged through the ankle-deep rice paddy mud. After I had been in the Army for maybe a year, I realized that our military had been training soldiers for nearly two hundred years; every aspect of training had a purpose.

Another experience that many remember vividly was the gas chamber. While being in the gas chamber did burn a bit until we put on and cleared our masks, it also taught us to follow instruction precisely. A DI, not the one in charge, would scream, "All clear; take off your mask." A number of men then took off their mask to the sudden sensation of tear gas and had to put the mask back on only to forget how to clear their mask. Some men even ran out of the gas chamber. Finally, the DI in charge would say, "All clear, remove your mask." The poor guys who had run out had to go back through the gas chamber as many times as it took to learn to listen to the man in charge. By the time we had finished with tear gas training, we all understood how serious following instructions was.

Most DIs had a great senses of humor. They would notice all of our mistakes, and often poke fun at our gaffes causing us to laugh under our breath, but also causing us to remember what they were teaching us. The following happened to a friend of mine early in his basic training. His DI, like many, would wake them at 0530 by beating on a trashcan. With this alarm, all jumped immediately out of bed and stood at attention in white tee shirts and boxer shorts. The DI walked past making sure all were present, up, and standing at rigid attention. On this particular morning, whether not thoroughly awake or just afraid to break his attention stance, this soldier stood there with his erect penis sticking out of his shorts. As the DI walked by each member of the platoon, all at attention, he said not a word nor broke step, he simply saluted the erect penis and kept on moving. All of those aware of what was happening were resolutely trying to hold back their laughter, for to laugh while at attention was a sure way to catch a severe butt-chewing. As soon as the DI saw all was well, he screamed, "Get to work ladies!" With the DI out of earshot, those who were able to see what had happened burst out in floor-rolling laughter. There are no words to express the embarrassment of that red-faced chap. Henceforth, his name was Pencil Dick. We experienced many hilarious events, all laughable but with us too intimidated to laugh aloud.

About halfway through our training, Sergeant Stulls sent me to the senior drill instructor. He said that the army was beginning a buildup and needed officers. Because of my high test scores, he wanted me to go through an interview for Officers Candidate School (OCS). I told him that if I had wanted to be an officer, I would have finished ROTC. I did not join the army to be an officer; I wanted to fight. He said that the army needed officers and that I would go for the interview, "Sergeant, yes, sergeant." I did, I was selected. I did not know that the number of people selected for OCS represented points for the senior DI; he intended to be the senior drill instructor of the top-rated company on graduation day.

There were at least two more such incidents aimed at helping him reach his goal. The next was on payday. We drew $78 a month. Before we went through the pay line, the senior DI said that we should all give $10 to the Red Cross. So, as we were paid we handed the company clerk $10. Later, the senior drill instructor congratulated us, for we not only had 100% participation, we gave the most of any training company. We all resented that. The senior DI pulled a third trick toward the end of training. At morning work call, the senior DI called out by name 15 or 20 of us. He told us to go back to our barracks, get a clean fatigue shirt and take it with us to the second platoon barracks. Meanwhile, he marched off the rest of the company. The company clerk led us to the second floor of the barracks and took up our shirts. We were to lie quietly on the floor until he came back. It would be several hours. When he came back, he gave us our shirts back; they were dirty. We rejoined the company. Later that evening when we were back in our barracks for the night, the men who had gone told us that ringers, people with our shirts on, took our PT tests for us. Our company did very well on its overall fitness rating. I did not know whether the senior DI was Phil Silvers' Sergeant Bilko or a crook. Either way, I knew the Army would not approve, but there was not a thing a Private E-1 could do about his charade.

On the other hand, Sergeant Stulls was a fine man. I never heard him swear or get upset. He genuinely cared about our learning and spent at least some time during the weeks of basic with each man. He certainly paid attention to my training. He took us from being the lowest form of humanity on the earth, buck privates, to being proud of what we accomplished in basic training. Except for the senior DI's antics, basic was fun. By the time we graduated, every man in our platoon had grown; we no longer referred to each other as "guys," we were now GIs.

Chapter 2: Training Gets Serious

I had been out of North and South Carolina only twice in my life. The enlistment posters at that time had a slogan printed on them: "Join the Army, See the World." After a short leave, it was off to California and Fort Ord for Advanced Infantry Training (AIT). I was thrilled. The army had given me travel pay and orders as to when and where to report. Therefore, I made my own travel arrangements, flew on a civilian aircraft to San Francisco, and stayed my first night in a motel near the airport. The next morning, I took the bus down the coast to Fort Ord. California, it was beautiful! Fort Ord fronted on one of the most scenic coasts in the United States. People spend millions to have houses along this shore. It did not cost me a cent to live in our WORLD WAR II-era barracks.

This was not basic training; there were no yellow footprints painted on the road here, and there were no DIs shouting at us. The DIs were platoon or master sergeants. My platoon had a master sergeant who had fought in WORLD WAR II, Korea, and Vietnam. He too was a soldier's soldier. His dress uniform had a ribbon rack that extended from the top of his blouse pocket to the edge of his epaulet plus a number of ropes and unit citations. The arms of his uniform had many enlistment slashes on its left arm and overseas bars on its right. Infantry training was far tougher than basic training. He pushed us, but we loved it. Virtually every man in our platoon was motivated. We learned.

Like Staff Sergeant Stulls, our platoon sergeant spent personal time with each of us. After more than 50 years, I am sorry, I cannot recall his name. He had three purple hearts and said that he wanted to make sure none of us got one. He emphasized the make-up of an infantry rifle squad and the job of each man in the squad. Our training was on the M-14 rifle and its fully automatic rifle version, the M14E2; the 1911 pistol; the M-79 Grenade launcher; the LAW anti tank rocket launcher; the hand grenade; the PRC-25 Radio; the M-60 machine gun; and the bayonet. Our platoon sergeant made sure we understood each weapon and what role that weapon played in the squad. He emphasized how we were to work together to maximize squad effectiveness in combat.

My WORLD WAR II father had told me to stay away from the machine gun because machine gunners were highly desirable targets and often did not last long in war, but one event caused me to fall in love with the M-60 machine gun. We were well along in our training and divided into reinforced squads when we went on our first ambush. Our platoon sergeant arranged us in an L formation parallel to a dirt road that was roughly L-shaped. The sergeant spread our men about ten feet apart facing the long part of the L; each positioned according to his role: riflemen, automatic riflemen (ARs), or grenadiers. Positioned near the end of the short part of the L with the gun pointed directly down the road was the machine gun. Our DI made sure we paid particular attention to our camouflage, because we would be well outnumbered and had to have the element of surprise. Each man was responsible for firing at targets to his immediate front. The machine gun was to fire down the road directly into the front of the main body of the oncoming soldiers. Our DI said that a machine gun firing into a line of soldiers, enfiladed fire, meant that the machine gun's bullets would likely penetrate four or five soldiers deep, taking them down and exposing the soldiers behind them to the next burst of fire.

All was quiet and hidden when an entire company of men came marching down the road, four abreast and maybe twenty-five deep, all in neat, straight lines. Once the company was beside the long arm of the L, the sergeant told me to fire. At that first machine gun burst, the entire squad opened up. Every man in that company had at least two weapons able to shoot him. I panned fire across the center of the chest of the first four leading men. I did it again and again. While we were firing blanks, we all saw how a well-planned ambush could devastate a much larger group of men. With the company in complete disarray, our squad quickly and quietly exited along pre planned routes. I loved it because the machine gun was by far the most devastating weapon in a rifle platoon. If this had been real, we would have killed or wounded many of the enemy, and all of us would have probably gotten away. In my youth, I had read much of John Singleton Mosby; here was one of his tactics only with modern weapons. Later, at the wrap-up, our sergeant explained that what we had done to that company was what the Viet Cong and North Vietnamese had been doing to our soldiers in Vietnam. It opened our eyes, for we all knew that Vietnam might well be the next place Uncle Sam planned for us to go: "Join the Army, See the World" – all of it.

We did not understand the why of so much detailed training. For example, our DI made us disassemble and reassemble our M-14s wearing a blindfold. He told us that when we reached our units, our platoon sergeants would assign each of us a specific weapon. Then we were to make sure that we learned to take that weapon apart and reassemble it blindfolded so that we would be able to repair it even in the dark or if blinded.

My first assignment when joining the 199th Light Infantry was that of assistant gunner on an M-60 machine gun weapons team. I did as the sergeant had said. It bailed us out four months later. On one black night in Vietnam, my gun jammed. I disassembled it in the black. I slid my fingers over the moving parts of the gun. I felt the broken parts. The roller bearing on the bolt had broken into several pieces blocking the bolt slide area. I knew the gun would fire without the bearing. I removed the broken remnants and quickly reassembled the gun and began to fight again. By daylight, fighting had broken off. I found that the little axle on which the bearing had been riding was damaged beyond repair, but the slide area was okay. We radioed for another bolt. A helicopter dropped the new bolt within two hours. That incident and others speak to the important job all DIs perform. I am thankful for them. When one is in training they may seem mean, but, in reality, they are angels.

Our training was great. This DI shared things that were not in our Field Manuals, things that certainly saved lives when we went to our war, things that were the products of his 20-plus years of service. In our second exposure to a gas chamber, our DI taught us that in a gas attack we were to take care of ourselves first, for we could not help others until we were able to function. Our DI explained that the same rule must apply when artillery, booby traps, or grenades wounded several of us at the same time. If wounded, we were to take care of ourselves first, then return to fighting or help our buddies; whichever was appropriate. I hoped I would never have to obey that rule. However, I did.

Soon after we moved just South of Saigon, the Mekong Delta area, two of us were wounded. Our gun crew consisted of Queen (the gunner), Newman (the ammo bearer), and me (Queens' assistant). Helicopters had just dropped our platoon off and a grenade exploded nearby. Queen was hit in the face and an eye. Newman was okay. I was hit in the groin. I wanted to help Queen, but I remembered our DI's instructions. I yanked my pants down and saw a number of small wounds. The largest was maybe three inches long. The bacon-sizzling sound I heard seconds before was me. The red-hot shrapnel had cauterized my wounds. I was more frightened than hurt. I sat down and, one at a time with my bare fingers, pulled all of the visible fragments from my wounds. We had a first aid pack. It contained an antiseptic-laced pad with four gauze ties. I applied the pad and tied the gauze tight. Meanwhile, the Lieutenant had called back one of the helicopters for a dustoff. Queen absolutely needed immediate help. I hoped he was not blind. The Lieutenant asked about me. "I'm okay. I'll carry the gun." Upon returning to base camp after our mission, the doctor treating me said that I was lucky, no infection. A few stitches, that was all. The Army never told us what happened to Queen. We assumed that Queen went home. Gardener became my assistant. He, Newman, and I made a darn good team. That DI's shared combat experience taught us the details of combat survival.

Our DI told stories that readied us for the kind of war Vietnam was. He said that guerrilla fighters were like mosquitoes; you could be outside enjoying yourself; then, a few of the tiny blood-sucking devils would show up and drive you nuts. No matter how hard you tried to swat them, they always moved just in time to be unscathed only to attack again. So it is with the Viet Cong. A few small units can keep an entire brigade busy.

Our DI used other analogies. "Dear John" letters broke more than one GI's heart. The regular soldier went home on leave to beat up the man who stole his girl only to land in jail. The guerrilla fighter would handle vengeance differently. When he went home, he would befriend the scoundrel – go fishing with him or to a ball game. He would learn the man's habits finding out that he would often come in drunk on Saturday nights and that he would leave a porch light on. There were bushes around his house. Then, one Saturday night, the guerrilla dressed in black and wearing a face mask, would unscrew the porch light bulb and hide in the bushes. When the man arrived home drunk enough to have trouble getting his key in the door lock, the masked man would quietly step out from behind the bush and beat John with a ball bat. The next day, the guerrilla fighter would be one of John's visitors saying, "John, what kind of animal would do something like this?" That is how a guerrilla is to think.

The roughest AIT training was escape and evasion. The entire company was marched to the base of a cliff, a part of the San Andreas Fault, where we waited until darkness. The senior drill instructor told us that when we got to the top of the cliff, we would be able to see the red light of a radio tower in the distance. If we went directly toward the red light, we would come to a bonfire; that fire marked friendly lines and safety. In the meantime, we would encounter the enemy. If caught, we wound be subjected to interrogation and torture. It would be best if we paired up.

The first obstacle was to climb the cliff in the dark. There were cuts in the cliff and much vegetation making that not too difficult. At the top, the enemy was waiting. They caught many of us. While my buddy and I got separated in the confusion, that same confusion gave us an opportunity to run. I had gone a few hundred yards and a man hollered, "Halt or I shoot!" I dove into some thick bushes hoping he would not see me. I quickly froze and forced myself to breath very shallowly. The man beat the bushes with his rifle. He did not stay long. He must have assumed that I had slipped away. I would not chance him simply waiting for me; I stayed completely still for what seemed like half an hour and then crawled to the edge of a large wooded area.

Later that night, I fell into a deep ditch. That fall knocked the breath out of me. After recovering for a few minutes, I heard a low voice say, "Are you okay?" It was my buddy. He helped me out of the ditch and we hugged each other. "How's it been going for you?" I whispered. He replied, "I damn near got caught but outran and out dodged the guy." "Have you been able to see the red light lately?" "Yes." He pointed in the direction of a tall tree a hundred or so yards to our front. "I have also heard trucks drive by to our left. I think it was the enemy taking their people back to form another line." We moved out quietly and did not run into any opposition. After several hours, we arrived at the bonfire. There we found a few other GIs who had already made it. A DI congratulated us and sent us back to our billets on a 3/4 ton truck. It was late so they let us sleep in. It was the evening meal of that day before they brought in the last of our company. They had walked all the way to Salinas and the radio tower. The soldiers that the enemy caught told of having to fold themselves into a wall locker that DIs beat on periodically. One man had honey poured on his head. Their miserable night lasted until first light and freedom. It does not sound like much now, but it fixed in our minds the idea that if captured, we would lose *all* control of what would happen to us. It made us never want to be captured.

One of the most frightening parts of our infantry education was bayonet fighting. On those days, we screamed over and over, "What is the spirit of the bayonet? To kill!" The idea was to make our adrenaline flow at the command, "Fix Bayonets." That training included how to use the rifle butt as a killing tool. Even though the bayonets were in their scabbards, it was too realistic. Yet, the most frightening training was our live-fire attack. While firing our M-14s, one squad at a time advanced uphill to a position on its top in a classic infantry assault. No blanks this time – real bullets. We not only had to fire as we moved, we had to learn to count our rounds, drop the empty magazine, and insert another. It was darn easy to get out of step. There were two DIs behind the ten of us keeping us in line so that we did not shoot one another.

During AIT, our ears often rang well into the night, for we spent plenty of time on firing ranges shooting different kinds of weapons. We also had to go through an obstacle course that ended with us crawling under barbed wire through mud with machine guns firing directly overhead and explosions going off throwing more mud on us. These events were more of a physical challenge than scary. It was exactly the correct preparation for where we would see plenty of live fire – Vietnam.

Overall, AIT was a great experience. Many of the men immediately got orders. I had to wait and so was assigned to work in the orderly room of one of the other training companies. The first sergeant there gave me the job of keeping up with all trainees and staff. That first sergeant was a character. For example, one day a malingerer came in with one of his excuses for wanting to miss that day's training. The first sergeant had him run to the mess hall to get a butcher knife and an onion. The onion had to be very large. When the soldier returned, the first sergeant took the onion, cut it in half and held one of the halves under each eye. He then said, "Tell me that story again so that I can cry." The entire orderly room broke out in laughter; that soon included the young soldier. He did not come back to the orderly room again.

We had all of our weekends off and had a ball in California. We went to San Francisco and its Haight-Ashbury district, the hippie section of the city. We were able to attend our first professional baseball game in uniform for free. Central California was beautiful, and we went often to Santa Cruz and Pebble Beach. Near there is Monterey, the Spanish capital of Baja (lower) and Alta (upper) California. We were able to see a sports car race at Laguna Seca raceway. We even got down to Big Sur. The Army had regular buses to these places, and we took advantage of that. Finally, my orders came down for airborne school. My first sergeant advised me not to go, for my OCS orders would be there soon. I hated that.

My orders did come down for OCS. I had a week's time-in-transit and then down to Fort Benning, Georgia. The first week of OCS was a review of my completed training. The second or third week, I received a phone call from Mother. My Father had had a severe heart attack and might not live. She wanted me to come home. I had her contact the Red Cross and the Army gave me an emergency leave. At home, my younger sister was away at college. In addition to Dad, Mom had my two brothers, one eleven and the other fourteen, to care for. Mother insisted that either she or I be with Dad around the clock. At that time, a severe heart attack meant lying flat on one's back and coming back slowly. Mom got my brothers off to school about 8 a.m. and had them stay with friends until time to cook supper, about 4:30 p.m. So, I was with Dad from 4:30 p.m. until 8 a.m.

Dad was not conversant the first few weeks, so we were rarely able to talk until the last of his fourth week in the hospital. During those few days, he spoke of his Army experiences. Dad enlisted in the summer of 1939. As part of the Lend-Lease deal with Great Britain, his coastal artillery unit was on an island near Trinidad when Pearl Harbor was bombed. His gun crew shot their 12-inch gun at some German submarines sinking one. Soon after that, he went to OCS. By the end of the war, he had become a battery commander in the coastal artillery.

At my last visit to his hospital room, he wished me well in OCS, but those four weeks of sitting with him for fifteen and a half hours a day had taken a toll on me. I went back to Fort Benning out of shape physically and mentally exhausted. I checked in with our first sergeant. He said that since I had been gone for four weeks, I would be assigned to another OCS company that was just beginning training. I told him that I was too exhausted to go through with OCS, and I really had joined the Army to fight. He said, "Are you sure?" I said, "Yes." He said he could send me over to the 199th Light Infantry Brigade after a bit of paperwork. They were going to Vietnam. I said yes. He sent me to the doctor to confirm my condition. A few days later, I was in my unit, soon to go fight.

Chapter 3: On to the 199th Light Infantry

A few days later, there I was in the Bravo Company (?), 2nd Battalion, 3rd Infantry Regiment (the Old Guard), 199th Light Infantry Brigade. The first sergeant there talked to me about my training and asked what I wanted to do. I said that I wanted to be on a machine gun crew. He sent me to the third platoon (?). Note: (?) means that I do not remember for certain.

The 199th had spent much time studying and training how to fight against guerrilla warfare. Indeed, my platoon sergeant told me that we were an experimental unit, a light and separate brigade. We had our own artillery, helicopters, and support. While in the service, I heard soldiers wonder why they got the assignments they did; did the Army know what it was doing? I saw firsthand that the Army knew exactly what it was doing: This experiential unit had a number of combat-experienced NCOs, and the officers were first class. I finally felt like I was in the Army.

My platoon sergeant, Staff Sergeant Rotten, had fought in Korea and spent time in a North Korean prison. He assigned me to Staff Sergeant Woollard, leader of the weapons squad. Over the next few weeks, Sergeant Rotten, Sergeant Woollard, and our platoon's two gunners helped bring me up to the training level of the unit. It tied in exactly with the training I had received at Fort Ord. Then it was home for two weeks' leave and back to Fort Benning. We then had a parade announcing our exiting Fort Benning and moving our colors to Vietnam.

First organized in 1784, the 3rd Regiment is the Oldest Infantry unit in the army. The 3rd is also the unit that guards Washington and the Unknown Soldier's Grave. We were the only group in the Army to march with fixed bayonets. Those bayonets are real and very sharp. During our parade at Fort Benning, one man was accidentally stabbed as we sat down on the parade field to hear our General speak. Our medics exited the man and treated him without missing a beat. The General delivered the speech as if nothing had happened.

The next day, we had our final inspection which was mostly about having the barracks, offices, and grounds clean, for all else was packed and ready. About 1500 hours, our platoon sergeant dismissed us with orders to be at a midnight formation. At midnight, our executive officer (XO) was standing in front of a formation of roughly 135 soldiers, most of whom were drunk. Rotten was not a drinker, but he too was pretty well loaded. A number of GIs were passed out and stacked like cordwood behind the formation. The XO called for reports. Sergeant Rotten staggeringly reported, "All present, Sir!" To that the XO responded, "Sergeant Rotten, you are not being a very good example for your men." Sergeant Rotten barked, "What do you mean, Sir? They are all drunk aren't they?" The formation roared with laughter.

We were up at 0500, quickly left Fort Benning and flew to Oakland California. The plane was quiet, for many of the hung-over soldiers slept the entire trip. We off-loaded our planes directly onto buses. The buses delivered us to the United States Army Transport Ship, a troop transport, the *Sultan*.

We embarked the next morning, a bright cloudless day. Going through the Golden Gate, seeing Alcatraz, San Francisco, its bay, and the California coast was an experience to cherish. It was stunning. Soon after we were out of sight of the shore, we hit a rough sea – rough for some who had never sailed. I stayed on the front end of the ship as it went up and down with spray coming back on me. It was great. As it was getting dark, I thought I had best go to quarters and started down the steps. I went by the first floor head. A few GIs were in there seasick. I went down to the next deck. Again, that head held nauseated, puking GIs. The smell hit me hard. It was that way until I reached the bottom of the ship where our quarters were, then I was in the head on my knees, my arms wrapped around the commode and my head resting on the commode edge. The commode edge felt so cool as I heaved my guts out. I did not eat that night or anything but nuts and soda crackers washed down only with water for the next three weeks; that was all I could hold down. English writer Samuel Johnson compared life on a ship to being in prison except "with the chance of being drowned." How do sailors live in these tight quarters rolling up and down day and night? My hat is off to them.

About halfway across the Pacific, we began taking four sulfur quinine tablets every Monday. They seemed nearly the size of a half dollar but thicker; you had to chew them up to be able to swallow them. They were the bitterest things I have ever put in my mouth. Sulfur quinine is an anti-malaria medicine. Later, after being in Vietnam, a number of us ended up with malaria symptoms anyway. That was after an unusually long helicopter flight headed west-north-west from our Vietnamese village. If we were not in Cambodia, we must have been on the border. Only the officers had map sheets, the only mission when that ever occurred. We, combat troops, had a recon mission in a pineapple plantation. We were only supposed to be there for a day but ended up in that hellhole for three days. We just carried one C-Ration box each and no bug juice (insect repellant). Resupply was not possible. We lived off the sweetest little pineapples any of us had ever tasted and drank rainwater from mud puddles. As soon as the sun set, mosquitoes covered us. They were thicker than the hair on our arms and maddening until the sun rose; then they disappeared to go get their rest for the next nightly attack.

About a week after returning, a number of us had flu-like symptoms accompanied by splitting headaches. The medic had nothing for us but more sulfur quinine. Though sick, the medics kept us in the field doing our jobs; that was the best way to keep our minds occupied, to tolerate the illness. Eventually the symptoms faded. I had several short bouts with those symptoms reappearing years later. Had the Army not started us eating those bitter tablets, our malaria symptoms would have been worse.

While on the ship, we had daily training and review sessions. We also had plenty of time to sit on the deck to read and talk. Indeed, one of the most valuable conversations of my life occurred on the deck. Queen, Newman, and I were talking to Sergeant Rotten. We asked him what was combat like? We were southern boys. So was he. He answered in terms we understood, "It's like hunting squirrels except the squirrels have rifles." We knew that squirrel hunting was a challenge. Living high up in the trees, squirrels heard and saw almost all that was going on. Always wary, they were nearly impossible to sneak up on. At the breaking of a twig or the rustling of leaves, the least sound, they retreated immediately up the nearest tree, to back side away from the sight of the hunter. There they quietly hid. We could imagine them having rifles, lying silently on a branch, senses keen, waiting on us with their weapons at the ready. Our training was thorough. We knew that the essence of guerrilla warfare was surprise. Squirrels usually had that. We knew that the only way to kill a squirrel was to be in the woods before first light and to sit completely still until they came out of their nest to eat just before sunup. Even then, you had to move decisively and slowly so as not to alarm them as you took aim and fired. We thought about that and talked about it until our first combat. Squirrel hunting is just like guerrilla warfare. The squirrels were to wound all three of us, Queen severely, Newman and me less so. Sergeant Rotten was right.

The pressure seemed to mount as we got closer to Vietnam; we had a tragedy. I do not know the man's name or anything about him; as I understood it, he took an air mattress and jumped overboard in the middle of the pacific. The ship circled for a couple of days looking for him or his body. No luck. That bothered us all.

Not all was business. We had some movies and at least one talent show. The talent was from the soldiers on board. There were GIs from Philadelphia who sang real street-level Do-Wop, a group that sang Rag Mop, and Doc Holiday who sang Rock-and-Roll along with other memorable talent. One gay GI danced to the music. He was the radioman for one of the company commanders and a darn fine soldier.

On the ship, I also got to know one of our platoon's most memorable characters, Spec 4 Willie Clyde Pitts. Before being drafted, Pitts was a barber at Pitt's Barber Shop, a family-owned business in Atlanta, Georgia. Through training in the field at Fort Benning, on the ship, and while in base camp in Vietnam, Willie Clyde kept our platoon's hair cut short for 50 cents a head. The Army had a reason for short hair; it gave lice and fleas fewer places to live. Pitts used hand-powered clippers, a comb, sharp scissors, and a straight razor to keep the fuzz on the top of our heads and our mustaches within regulations. One of the few people known by his

civilian name, when you sat in front of Willie
Clyde, be it on a five-gallon can or an empty ammo
crate, you were back home in his overstuffed
barber's chair. "How's it going, Sergeant Allen?"
"I got a dear John letter from my girl this week."
"That's horrible." "What did she say?" "Willie
Clyde, she is going to marry my best friend."
"That's dirty. You are over here fighting and they
do you like that. What are you going to do?"
"When I get home, I'm going to find that bastard
and whip his ass!" "Sergeant, it's only been three
months since you left. He is not your friend and she
can't be much either. You go home fighting and
you'll end up in jail, and for what, for two skunks.
Maybe you're better off to get your mind straight."
The sergeant knew that Willie Clyde was right.
Willie was part psychologist and every man's friend
except Guyton's. Spec 4 Guyton was also from
Georgia, and for some reason, Willie Clyde could
not pass Guyton without some sarcastic words. I
never understood how Clyde could help so many but
not help himself.

While we slept, we arrived at Okinawa.
Charge of Quarters (CQ) awakened me at 0200. I
had bakery duty. The ship was still for the first time
in weeks, and, for the first time in weeks, I was not
seasick. Every time I took a baking sheet full of
cinnamon buns out of the oven, I had one. I even
ate breakfast.

Not long after breakfast they off-loaded us
from the ship and marched us to a military post's
club where Japanese singers entertained us singing

American songs. Most ordered steaks. I had a seafood platter. There was much beer drinking, it was a celebration to be off that cussed ship. Soon, many were half drunk, so the ranking officer decided he had better get us back on board while all were still able to march. Away we staggered, trying to keep in step. Back at the ship, the entire brigade was standing in formation on one side of the pier waiting to board; many had to take a leak. Suddenly, someone broke ranks, ran to the other side of the pier and started pissing on the ship! Almost instantly, the entire formation, more than a thousand GIs, broke ranks and with tens of gallons of spent beer painted the ship. This act showed what Infantry thought of shipboard life.

It was then off to Vietnam where I never saw any heavy drinking. The heavy drinking before leaving Fort Benning and the event just mentioned were the only such incidents I saw while in the Army. These men were America's finest and not given to excess; both of these events were due to the uncertainty a troop of brothers felt knowing that they would soon face combat. Combat would be too serious for any high-spirited mischievous activity and we knew it.

Chapter 4: First Actions

We arrived in late November, Vietnam's dry season. There were three advantages to having crossed the Pacific on a ship. Two were the time, a twelve-hour time difference from Fort Benning, and the temperature, which would be in the high nineties. We had pretty well adapted to those conditions as they slowly changed crossing the Pacific. The third advantage was that the time on the ship also gave us a chance to review and discuss our training and tactics.

On our last full day aboard ship, Uncle Sam paid us in military scrip. It looked like Monopoly money. We would only receive $50 a month while in Vietnam. The army would hold back the balance of our pay until we left Vietnam. The idea of both the military script and the reduced take-home pay was to help keep the American presence from upsetting the Vietnamese economy. However, we were to find that the Vietnamese took our military script without hesitation.

Supply then issued us jungle fatigues and jungle boots. These jungles fatigues fit loosely for airflow and were made of light-tightly-woven cotton poplin for sun protection. The boots were leather in the foot area with nylon uppers; they had vent holes in the arch area and woven nylon sole inserts to help with airflow. In addition, the boots' woven nylon sole inserts and nylon sides provided some protection against punji stick booby traps. The punji stick booby trap is a simple hole, two to three feet deep by two feet in diameter. At the bottom of the hole were sharpened wood or bamboo sticks with the sharpened end facing up. They also had sharpened sticks on sides of the hole facing down at roughly a sixty-degree angle. The Viet Cong (VC) dug these punji holes in a path concealing them under small sticks and leaves. They looked like the path and ground around it. A soldier would unknowingly step on the hole; instantly his entire body weight would fall on one foot the sharpened sticks stabbing that foot. The soldier would try to extricate his pained foot only to impale his leg on the sharpened side sticks. The enemy often defecated on the sticks in hopes of infecting the wounds they caused. The simple punji stick booby traps were effective in taking a man out of combat, and slowing a unit until a helicopter evacuated the wounded man. Jungle boots were our foot armor.

Just before we put on our jungle uniforms, Sergeant Rotten told us that we would not need underwear or socks in this hot climate. Underwear and socks would stay wet with sweat – a great place for bacteria and fungus to grow. We were not to wear any rank or unit insignia, for such might give the enemy useful information. We each put our regular fatigues, underwear, and so forth in our duffel bags. A transport boat would take them ashore. We arrived in Vietnam that night.

Early the next morning, supply gave us our weapons and a basic load of ammo. The rope ladders went over the ship's side as the landing craft pulled up. We inserted full magazines in our weapons but did not chamber a round. We slung arms and climbed down the ladders in full battle gear. We climbed into LCM-8 landing crafts. They looked much like WORLD WAR II Higgins boats only larger. The boats moved us quickly to the shore where a number of us kissed the ground; we loathed life aboard the ship. It would be fifty-years before anyone got me aboard another ship; that was a Disney Cruise our son-in-law and our youngest daughter gave my wife and me as a gift.

There was a convoy of deuce-and-a-halves waiting on us. The transport crew had piled our duffel bags in the middle of a dirt road. The first platoon's platoon sergeant said since all of our duffel bags were there, just grab one and take it on a truck with you. We would sort them out later. That was the only time while I was in the army that each person did not carry his own gear, a mistake that later cost me. As we rode through the country, I was amazed both at the beauty of the jungle forest and the poverty of the villagers.

We arrived to find that the advance team, who had flown over, had set up tents and cots. Immediately after we got off the trucks, we began sorting our duffel bags. We found all except for mine. My platoon sergeant told me to put in for a replacement; I did. A few weeks later, a supply officer told me that I should have kept up with my own gear. I explained that I was doing what the sergeant in charge told us to do; that was no excuse in the officer's eyes. That meant that I had to buy all new underwear, socks, boots, fatigues, hats, a field jacket, and an overcoat after I left Vietnam on the way to Germany. I had learned in Basic Training that privates were bottom feeders; it was the same for a PFC. I resented that.

Our first camp was somewhere near Long Binh. There were no floors in the tents and the dirt floors soon turned to mud. We were able to find some shipping skids to put beside our cots to help keep our bare feet clean. Most guys purchased some footlockers from the Vietnamese. They were made of thin wood covered with bright thin sheet metal. By the end of our first day, we were settled in only to have our first mission the second day.

Our first mission: Engineers were clearing a large area of jungle nearby. They drove huge bulldozers with a 50-caliber machine gun mounted beside the drivers on each. We were to look for snipers who had been targeting the engineers. We went to the farthest point of the engineers' work area where the remains of the jungle still stood. It was not the beautiful jungle we had seen riding in on deuce-and-a-halves from the ship. As far as we could see, there were groups of holes caused by artillery fire. The holes, roughly twenty-five by thirty feet by three feet deep, were partly filled with groundwater. On the water floated a thin film of what looked like oil. Snapped and splintered trees surrounded each hole. There were no leaves on the trees, not even a blade of grass. Defoliants (Agent Orange) had bared all of what the artillery had not wasted. Save for the blue sky above, all was black and gray and dead. Surely, this is the way the gates of hell look.

That mission was uneventful. Late in the evening of the next day, we were part of three large circles made of hundreds of soldiers in the jungle, one circle within the other. We were in the outermost of the circles that was miles in diameter. At the center of the circles was the Bob Hope Christmas show; this was but one stop on his Southeast Asia tour. The objective was to keep the audience safe from attack. We did not get to see Bob Hope. However, we were near a village that must have had a Roman Catholic Church, for we could hear singing in Vietnamese. We recognized the music of *Silent Night*. It moved us to tears. For most of us young soldiers, this Christmas season would be the first spent away from home; we were sad.

The next day, we received our first mail since leaving the States. Mom had sent me some oatmeal cookies that shipping and handling had beaten into crumbs. The crumbs tasted great. Dad understood the importance of letters; I got several letters from him all encouraging but also showing that he did fear for me. One high school girlfriend had sent me a note; she realized that she did not love me. Letters were our only way of communicating with home; I wrote every chance I got to every girl whose address I had or could obtain. As I began to get responses, I learned that without the facial expressions and voice tones of verbal communications, humor and sarcasm are nearly impossible to recognize. If you ever write a GI, do not ask him what he is doing that is dangerous; it will make you look stupid. Do not ever say, "I'll see you in heaven."

Later that same day, we moved into the jungle in company strength. There had been no defoliant used here. Our training had emphasized being quiet and not bunching up. Yet, here we were, 120 men in a tight, noisy line hacking our way through bamboo three inches in diameter with machetes, an ideal target for an ambush by the enemy. Perhaps the only thing that saved us was the thickness of the jungle. The stout bamboo grew side by side, so close that a grown man could not slip between them.

Later that evening, exhausted, we cut firing lanes and bedded down. To relax, some guys made cups and canteens out of the bamboo. As night set in, one member of our machine gun crew would have to be awake at all times. We took turns an hour at a time. We quickly realized that that was no way to get any meaningful sleep. Hence, we learned to divide the night into three evenly spaced watches. The rest of my time in Vietnam, I had the middle watch.

The south of Vietnam is close to the equator so the amount of daylight varies little year round. Further, this part of Vietnam had only two seasons, wet and dry. Wet season was from May through October and the dry season was from November through April. It poured rain almost every day during the wet season and it rarely rained in the dry season. All seasons were hot.

However, one weather event was among the most painful of my Vietnam experiences. The hot sun had the temperature well into the nineties. We had just finished a mission and called for helicopters to pick us up. The helicopters did not come. Instead, we found ourselves out in the open and under a severe thunderstorm. The cold rain mixed with pea-sized hail poured down on us for what seemed like twenty minutes. That ice-cold mix of rain and hail on top of our hot sweaty bodies was painful. The only thing that we could do was to wait with our backs to the wind. My right shoulder locked up. The only part of our bodies that made out okay was that part of our heads under our helmets. It's funny, among all of the times I was in combat, I remember this weather event powerfully.

Back to our fifth day in country, we hacked a path through the jungle until late afternoon. There we found a small, low hill where the jungle growth was not as thick as what we had chopped through all day. At the foot of the hill was an old road. The company formed up into defensive positions around the top of the hill. Our platoon had the clearest side of the hill. On this same hilltop, the 4th Infantry had fought a battle a year before. Our Commanding Officer (CO or Old Man) sent out squads to reconnoiter. Assigned to support the first squad of our platoon, we carried our gun down the hill to the old road. We followed the road as it went up a low hill.

As we moved along, we heard an occasional man scream; he sounded like a panther. In training, we had learned that that was how the Viet Cong (VC or Charlie) sometimes drew Americans into an ambush. Our squad leader radioed that information back. All of the noise the company made hacking through the jungle had to have alerted the enemy. Now, we were one squad alone. We were anxious. A few minutes later, our platoon leader radioed telling us to stay the night where we were. There was little time to look for a good ambush site. We moved back down the road to a flat area. We set up a few feet off the road and along a creek bank. The creek's width was maybe six feet. The creek's banks were five or six feet nearly straight down to the shallow water of a creek. This creek was like a long winding trench, an ideal place for soldiers to find shelter from both small arms fire and artillery explosions. We also knew that creeks often served as roads in the jungle. We were justifiably tense.

Not too long after complete darkness, we heard people walking in the creek. We opened fire. Grenades were going off, some ours in the creek and some theirs around our position. Newman lay just to my right. Grenade shrapnel slashed into his nose. He was a little bloody but okay. Off and on, it was like that all night. It was frightening. Our gun had fired over 500 rounds that night. However, we had set up in a poor position. The creek zigzagged; that and its trench shape made us completely ineffective. Lesson: If there is not enough time to survey your surroundings, call back requesting a move back the trail already traveled to a stronger position. Further, this soldier thought fear was a bad thing; it is not. It is uncomfortable but vital. It enables one to stay highly alert for hours on end.

Soon after first light, the CO ordered us back to the main group on the hill. We set our machine gun up on edge of an old foxhole, a foxhole likely dug by members of the 4th Infantry Division during a battle a year prior. The area immediately in front of our hole was relatively clear giving us a good view down on much below. Banks, one of our medics, removed the shrapnel from Newman's nose and put a rather large bandage on it. The Old Man called in an Air Force spotter plane. The next thing we knew, a P-51 painted in South Vietnamese colors showed up. The spotter plane fired a rocket marking the spot where he saw the enemy and that Mustang flew figure eights passing back and forth over the place the spotter had marked. The Mustang's machine guns were blazing and he let off his rockets. The Mustang left and the spotter returned to the area. Soon an F-4 Phantom showed up. There was no zigzag, no figure eights, with this fast monster. It passed over only to zoom out of sight. Again, the spotter let loose another rocket marking the enemy's position. The F-4 came back to see where to attack. Again, he zoomed out of sight. When he returned, we could see his bomb leave the plane. It glided down exactly on the place marked. The bomb blast shook the ground and a large piece of shrapnel landed beside Queen. We sprang into action using our helmets to dig our hole deeper just in case the Phantom came back and dropped another bomb. It did not return. We were ordered to go to where we had spent the night and report. Other squads went to the bombsite.

All of our machine gun brass was gone. On returning to our hill position and reporting, Sergeant Rotten told us that our 7.62 x 51 brass would work in the enemies Nagant rifles and carbines. By only elongating and reshaping the neck of our brass, they would have their 7.62 x 54 brass. That is, they could reload our brass and use it on us. The other squads reported that the 500-pound bomb had done its work. Some shredded, muddy, bloody body parts were up in the trees and on the ground around the bomb crater. Among the carnage, they found a foot that had a Chinese boot on it and part of a Chinese officer's uniform on a torso. There must have been an enemy advisor traveling with the VC. Lesson: War is beyond brutal; it is horrifying.

We spent the night back up on the hill. With this first combat, the invincibility of our youth left us. We knew that we could die. We knew that our buddies could die. The squirrels do have rifles, but we have 500-pound bombs.

The next morning, we returned to the thick jungle and again hacked our way along. About mid-day, we heard an explosion. Our line stopped. The Executive Officer (XO) came back down the line borrowing machetes. The Old Man was near the front of our long line of soldiers weaving its way through the jungle. As he moved along, brush had somehow grabbed the pin of one of his grenades on an ammo pouch and it had gone off. It had done great damage to him. Directly behind him, his radio operator also received ghastly wounds. The borrowed machetes were to be used to clear a place where a medical evacuation helicopter (a dustoff) could land to take the two to a hospital. We never knew what happened to the Old Man or his radio operator. Our DIs in AIT taught us how to attach grenades on an ammo pouch to help avoid what had happened to our CO. The CO was a West Pointer and fine officer, but he must have missed that in training. The XO took command, and for the next few weeks, we hacked and cut trail after trial in that area.

During these remaining time in the jungle, we soldiers found that we fought more than the hot climate and the opposition army; there were health concerns rarely faced in America. One of our tallest soldiers felt something in his penis. He unbuttoned his trousers and saw the tail end of a leech hanging out of the hole in the end of his manhood. He let loose a loud terrified scream, "Medic!" By the time the medic got through the thick growth of the jungle, the soldier was almost in shock as the leech had crawled up into him. The medic had no idea what to do. The medic called the head medic and he came. He did not know what to do either. They radioed back to a doctor who told them it was nothing to worry about; the leech would eventually die and be expelled in the soldier's urine. That was no help to the soldier. He wanted that damn leech out of him. Sorry, the doctor said, "You will be alright." His platoon leader then told the soldier that he would have to wait until we got back to a base camp to see a doctor. "Keep on soldiering." The poor man was a nutcase for the remaining time in the jungle.

Most of us did not take even our boots off during our time in the jungle. Ducking down into a creek as we crossed it was the nearest thing we had to a bath. We returned to a base camp to first clean our weapons, shower, scrub our nasty selves, and change our filthy clothes. We all also found some masking tape and taped our grenade pins just for a bit more grenade safety.

The General came out to present us with our Combat Infantry Badges. He was most complimentary, ending his speech with, "You all need to get a little closer to a razor." You see, virtually every man had trimmed his three-week growth of beard into everything from fancy pork chop sideburns to goatee mustaches to full beards. The General wanted these facial decorations trimmed to military regulation. We felt great but we did not fool ourselves; we knew there was more to learn; we just had no idea how much. We did cut our hair decorations back to regulation but kept our moustaches. You see, our helmet protected our heads from the sun but our upper lips, noses, ears and the backs of our necks were constantly sunburned and peeling. Moustaches protected our upper lips from the sun.

It was about then that we got another moral boost. We started receiving *The Stars and Stripes*, a newspaper for GIs published by the Department of Defense. We always read it from cover to cover. It was usually upbeat but honest. I particularly liked its comic book illustrations. *The Stars and Stripes* was as important as were letters from home. We trusted the paper; that is more than I can say about a piece I saw on CBS's *60 Minutes* shortly after returning to the States. Filmed about the 199th just before I rotated from Vietnam to Germany, it was a total misrepresentation. For example, they interviewed two buck privates. These were not combat soldiers; they were peeling potatoes. They were anti-war. Years later, I learned that communists like Pham Xuan An did a great job of making GIs look like we were losing the War, and made us look like baby killers. This communist' plant was a correspondent for *Time, Reuters,* and the *New York Herald Tribune.*

Chapter 5: The Mekong River Delta, an Education

We were back on deuce-and-a-halves headed to our new location somewhere south of Saigon. Our new commanding officer was the finest officer I ever met. He explained to us that we were part of a group of allies: Americans, South Koreans, Australians, Filipinos, New Zealanders, Siamese, Taiwanese, and Canadians. The enemy was composed of Viet Cong, North Vietnamese, Chinese, Soviets, North Koreans, and Cubans. Our part of the war was to be in the Mekong River Delta. The Delta covers almost one-fourth, more than 15,000 square miles, of South Vietnam producing three crops of rice a year. The communist nations, particularly the Chinese, were backing the North Vietnamese and the Viet Cong (VC) so that they would have access to the Delta's abundant rice production. This was not a civil war; this war was about *RICE*.

In the Delta, the VC had run off or murdered the doctors, teachers, nurses, and any educated Vietnamese; they only wanted that part of the population that grew and processed rice. The VC drafted farm boys and very young men, often at the tip of a bayonet. They killed anyone who dared stand against them. Their training focused on guerrilla warfare and on being a loyal communist. The Cold War had caused our Army to prepare to fight the Soviets in Europe. There, holding territory was the objective. The VC cared little about whose territory they fought on. We were so married to the Cold War model of warfare that we were not prepared to fight the guerrilla warfare raging in Vietnam.

We had tremendous transportation advantages, powerful artillery and hundreds of helicopter gunships. The tactic used by the VC in the Delta to overcome these powerful advantages: They ambushed us only when they were so close to us that we could not call in artillery or helicopter gunships for fear of killing ourselves. They would wound or kill a few of us quickly and fade away as near instantly as was humanly possible. The aim of the 199th's training: use new tactics aimed at combating this close and personal kind of warfare. We were now too engaged in Operation Fairfax. The old tactic of WORLD WAR II and Korea, hold and protect your territory, was out the window. Our new tactic: search out the enemy and destroy him where he was. The CO was quite clear, it was here in the Delta that our Company was to test this new tactic; we were the guinea pigs. Here we would do battle.

Our first stop was a small village surrounded by rice paddies. Our company quickly circled the village and took up positions. Attached to a squad located at a village corner, our machine gun crew had a 270-degrees view. At our backs was the village. To our front, we could see miles of dry rice paddies. Spread across the rice paddies every few inches was rice plant stubble. Crisscrossing the rice paddies every few hundred yards were creeks edged with thick growths of Mekong River Palms.

These Mekong River Palms edged most of the Delta's rivers and creeks. This dwarf palm is a hardy plant whose roots are able to stand the strong, rushing current of the tidal waters. The plants' flexible stems do not snap under the currents' pressures. They usually grew so close together that they formed a thicket in which we learned to hide and ambush VC.

The villagers behind us were friendly, even festive; the harvest was in and would soon be at the market. The villagers had large tarps, maybe 20 feet long, spread on the ground in front of almost every house. There were two piles of rice, one at each end of their tarps with a much smaller pile of chaff set in the middle. The villagers were taking turns using large wooden shovels to throw the rice up in the air from one pile to the next. The rice grains, being heavier than the chaff, made it to the pile on the other end of the tarp. The chaff landed in the middle; occasionally a child swept it away. The villagers threw the rice from one pile to the next, back and forth, until there was only rice. They then sacked that for market.

The villagers' homes were of interest. They had a log and stick frame covered with thatch, Mekong River Palm. The thatch was five or six inches thick, each piece being roughly 6 feet long. Turned face side up, the leaves formed flattened V-shaped troughs. These little leaf troughs carried the rainwater down the roofs to gutters made of large bamboo split in half with all bamboo baffles removed. Below the end of each bamboo gutter was a large terracotta barrel. The creek and river water not being potable, the people drank this barreled rainwater. The interior of the homes were great protection against the hot sun letting air flow freely. They had hard-packed dirt floors.

All of our communication with the Vietnamese was via hand signs, for none of us knew their language and they knew no English. However, by the time work that day was ending, we were laughing with the farmers and soon leg wrestling with some of the men. Their leg wrestling was akin to our arm wrestle. A GI would lay on his back with a Vietnamese parallel but with his head in the opposite direction. On the count of one, two, and on three, the GI and Vietnamese fellow would lock legs and see who could overcome his opponent.

As evening came, the villagers went into their homes, and we ate our C-rations (Cs) and repositioned ourselves a hundred yards or so from the village edges behind dikes. The dikes were only four or five inches high but provided some cover. Those of us not on the first watch slept well.

However, when awakened for the second watch, we were laying in three or four inches of water. With the rice harvest complete, it was time to re-flood the rice paddies. The Vietnamese open holes in the dikes. The South China Sea's high tide pushes the fresh water of the Mekong River back into the Delta and that rising tide floods the rice paddies. At high tide, the paddies are full and the villagers close the holes in the dikes holding the water for the next rice planting.

They would use this method to keep their fields flooded for several months while they planted the rice and grew it to maturity. Then they would open the dikes to let the low tide and fast river currents pull the water out of the paddies, close the dikes, and let the fields dry readying them for harvest.

This is all possible due to the flatness of the Mekong River Delta and the South China Sea's 12-foot tides at the mouth of the Mekong River. This powerful tide reversed the flow of the River, having an amazing effect on the Delta's waterways and making it an ideal place for rice paddies. The highest point in Delta's 15,000 square miles was less than 10 feet above sea level letting the effects of the tide extend fifty miles inland up the Delta's rivers and creeks.

The map of our current area, a 1:28,000 scale, had only one contour line and that contour line increment was one foot. Over hundreds of years, the Vietnamese had turned the Delta's swampland into a giant rice garden. Knowing the timing of the tides was the key to the farmers controlling the water levels of their fields. To us soldiers, the timing of the tidal water was also important. Mid tide to high tide and back to mid tide was the time of river traffic, the primary transportation for Delta people. We learned that high tide near midnight made the ideal night for the VC to pole and paddle their sampans full of supplies and fighters around the

Delta's waterways, the highways of the Delta. That made it the best time for us to bushwhack the VC.

The speed of the tide was another significant factor. The Mekong River, during peak tidal flow, reached a speed of more than a yard a second. It was three times that speed on some of the smaller rivers and creeks. That fast tidal flow made the Delta's rivers and creeks often treacherous. My platoon lost one man to drowning, PFC Locklear, a darn nice soldier and member of the Lumbee Nation from the Pembroke area of North Carolina.

The next day, we received our first Sundries packages (goodie boxes). They contained cigarettes, soap, gum chuckles, Hershey tropical chocolate bars, razors, shave cream, paper, pens, envelopes and other stuff that we would have purchased at the Post Exchange (PX) if back in the States. I did not smoke and so swapped my share of cigarettes for soap knowing that I had seen the ladies of the village washing their clothes and their children just using elbow grease.

My thinking was that I would give my soap to the Vietnamese ladies who had children. We then had a little time to see the inside of the two or three shops in the village. In one, I found the black silk cloth from which the villagers made their clothes. Their clothes looked like black silk pajamas. I asked the lady who ran the shop to make me a set of those silk pajamas. I figured they might come in handy going to and coming from an ambush. She did and had them ready the next day. I motioned to her, "How much?" She knew we GIs had soap, and we settled on a price – three bars of goodie box soap. Her huge smile told me that she was thrilled with that deal. I gave the other bars away as planned. Few Americans realize how blessed we are.

Sergeant Hathaway, a large native Hawaiian, found a set of camouflage jungle fatigues like the South Vietnamese Rangers wore. He bought those with soap. They blended in with the palm thickets but faded after several washings. Later, a few other soldiers purchased some of the same fatigues. In the States, we would not have dared to be in such clothes, be out of uniform, but here, let's try it.

Chapter 6: Close Combat and the Enemy Takes Casualties

After a few days, we moved to another village a few miles further into the Delta. That would be our home for the rest of my time in Vietnam and our introduction to serious combat. This village, Long Doc, was much larger than the last. Divided into two parts of roughly equal size, a steel bridge crossing a river was the center. We occupied the northern half.

Buddhism was the dominant religion in Vietnam. When we had time to walk around this village, we saw a few Buddhist monks with their shaved heads and dressed in their bright red and yellow robes. They lived in a small pagoda, their monastery. The monks left and gave our platoon use of the pagoda. Several of us were to live there. That was not our only new experience.

We humans have many ways of disposing of sewage. Those Vietnamese living in villages had a unique, one might say ecologically friendly, way of disposing of theirs. They built their privies over ponds. One pond typically served several homes. When using the privy, the feces and urine fell into the pond. There, catfish swirled around excited, ready to eat the waste. Periodically, the villagers lowered the pond's water level at low tide. Then several of them waded through the pond using seines to catch the larger catfish leaving the smaller ones to grow. They would then refill the pond at high tide. For those Vietnamese living near a river, they built their privies over the rivers. The villagers considered catfish a delicacy. Personally, this American soldier no longer eats catfish.

Then, a good thing happened. The engineers erected two platform tents in the center of our half of the village. One tent was a headquarters for the CO and immediately beside that was a mess hall – how wonderful! After living off Cs for more than a month, we would get real food. The Army had some darn great cooks.

The engineers then erected four other platform tents, one roughly in the center of each platoon's area of responsibility plus one for our supply sergeant. The CO wanted us soldiers spread out in the village so that the enemy would have the fewest possible soldier-dense targets. The platoon leaders, platoon sergeants, and radio operators occupied the tents. Some fire teams rented unoccupied Vietnamese houses. Others occupied a small Buddhist temple. Some of our platoon also occupied a triangular dried mud fort on the northeastern corner of the village. Built by the locals, the walls were maybe four feet high, eight feet thick at the base narrowing to four feet across the top of the wall. The interior triangular fort was roughly fifty feet by fifty feet by fifty feet. Firing positions were each of the three corners of the fort. The dried mud was almost like concrete and provided good protection against small arms fire. Surrounding the village were rice paddies crisscrossed by creeks edged by a six-to eight-foot thick growth of Mekong River Palms. The palms' growth was a bit wider along the river than along the creeks.

From the first night, squads from each platoon were patrolling during the day, finding and occupying ambush positions by night. Maybe a mile from the village, the squad we were assigned to found a great position for a typical L-shaped bushwhack, in this case a backwards L along a creek. The last 100 feet of the creek flowed straight with a hook of land where the creek fed into a river. The little hook at the end of the creek was where we would set up our machine gun pointing it back up the creek. The creek was maybe twelve feet wide and small sampans were maybe four feet wide. Any sampans traveling the creek would likely be poling down the center of the creek.

At high tide, the little hook of land would be but inches above the water line. Therefore, our gun's bipod held its barrel less than a foot above the creek. This was a machine gunner's dream, all of the enemy on a flat surface headed directly for our position in a straight line: concentrated flat trajectory enfilade fire. Queen and I were most concerned with one thing: not shooting our men on the right bank in the black of night.

We would concentrate our first and heaviest fire down the center of the creek. As the bullets blew to pieces the thin-hulled wooden sampans, the enemy would not be able to return fire. They would likely jump and swim toward the left bank away from our men. That is where we would spread our secondary fire. The squad then lined up its ten men over roughly the last sixty feet of the creek. Preston, a grenadier, would be at the farther end of the squad and would be the one to quietly alert us and start the ambush by shooting off a flare. Sergeant Hathaway radioed our coordinates to our artillery in case we needed fire support. It was all set.

We moved a few hundred yards away from the area, relaxed and ate our Cs. We were waiting for sunset. Soon after sunset, we quietly moved back into our positions along the creek's edge and the cover of the Mekong Palms. I had a 200-round belt hooked to our gun with four more cans of ammo (800 more rounds) to my left. Queen and I had a good view of our squad's position. Newman was maybe six feet to Queen's right and able to communicate with the rest of the squad. As darkness fell, the tide was inbound. No one slept. All were hyper-alert.

Queen had been in the prone position on the gun since dark fell. To his left, I was on one knee, my head three feet higher than was his but able to see little for not much moon and starlight shown through the thick palm growth on both sides of the creek. Then it happened. We heard the sound of the boats and poles as the enemy moved through the water. Nerves on edge, Newman tapped Queen's boots – that was the ready signal. Preston shot a flare (M-127); we let hell loose. Adrenaline flowed, normally a machine gun fires bursts of six rounds and then the gunner takes aim again, but Queen fired about a hundred rounds, ten or twelve seconds' worth, all straight down the creek. I could see by the blaze of our weapons firing that the bullets exploded the sampans as men fell. "Do it again," I whispered to Queen. He let loose ten to twelve round bursts again and again, not only up the creek but also up the left bank.

I had already hooked another 200 rounds on and the gun had eaten some of them. Newman had also emptied several magazines from his M-16 on full auto as had every rifleman in the squad. The grenadiers were firing up the creek, their rounds exploding brightly. Hathaway shouted, "Hold your fire! Grenadiers, fire flares. Everyone, look for targets!" The two grenadiers fired their M-79's flares, one man and then the other. Nerves on edge, visible were parts of boats, bullet broken palm branches and a few bodies floating along on the strong inbound tide. Hathaway checked; we were all okay. We all fired sporadically as we saw anything that might be an enemy. Newman brought over another two cans of ammo (400 rounds). It was but a short time before the artillery flares Hathaway called lit the area bright as day. They did this for hours. Hathaway radioed back. Word came down the squad, "Stay alert. The Old Man will be here soon after first light."

The CO, with thirty or forty men, swept in. The CO positioned his men in defensive positions on each side of the creek. His first words to us were, "As we came over, we found twelve fresh mud grave mounds some on each side of the creek above that dogleg." He was pointing back toward the dogleg in the creek.

We stayed put answering the Old Man's questions while the group he had with him began searching the area. It was then back to the village to restock our ammo, refill our canteens, and clean our weapons. The CO had the mess hall opened with eggs, sausage, bacon, steaks, pancakes, milk, juice, great Army coffee, and then we slept.

That night we stayed in the village and reviewed the ambush. We had to wonder, if we killed twelve, how many did we wound or was our fire so devastating all in front of us died? The strong rising tide had been inbound enabling the enemy up the dogleg to pick up their dead, but how many healthy enemies were there? Gathering twelve dead and burying them before first light was not the work of a small group. It is likely that we took the enemy totally by surprise; that must have disoriented them, for a large group could certainly have counterattacked. It is a good thing that artillery flares turned the night to day as long they did. Surely, no enemy would advance in a lighted battlefield unless the target was worth lives. They probably would have been too close for us to call in exploding artillery or gunships. Overall, the ambush went well. Lessons learned: Flares are wonderful. Never underestimate the enemies' strength. Always, prepare for counterattack. Our biggest mistake: we did not call in exploding artillery further up the creek to possible enemy locations safely beyond our ambush.

I had to wonder about the dead enemy. The VC probably forced at least some of them into the Viet Cong against their will. They were human beings. Killing a farm boy or young man is the ultimate contraceptive; you stop all he could have been. No children will be born to remember him as father or grandfather. He had two parents and before them, there were four grandparents and eight great grandparents and on back. All must be heartbroken. Is that bloodline finished? If there is an afterlife, I would hope that I could meet the men I helped kill and be friends with them as they can meet the men they killed and be friends with them. In this close and personal kind of combat, I felt both tremendous excitement and revolting horror.

Chapter 7: We Continue to Learn

First, a few words about helicopters, for they were the principle way we traveled to where the enemy was. Our helicopter assaults occurred in two ways: the helicopter would drop down like a fast-falling elevator on the target or we would come in at treetop level. Most of those assaults were on Huey UH-1 transport helicopters and a few on Chinook CH-47s. The Huey had a crew of four: two pilots and two door gunners. The two pilots were a Warrant Officer who typically flew the Huey and a Lieutenant to his side who did the navigating. The two machine gunners fired covering fire as we assaulted our target of the day.

In addition to the Huey transport helicopters, there were Hueys with red crosses painted on them to dust off our wounded. They carried stretchers and medics along with medical supplies. They would treat our wounded while in flight. Then there were short-bodied Huey gunships for ground-support fire. The armament aboard Huey gunships typically included a traversable M-134 Minigun with six rotating barrels that could fire 6,000 rounds per minute; a rocket launcher on each side of the helicopter both carrying seven 2.75-inch folding-fin rockets; a .50-caliber machine gun and a 7.62-mm M-60 machine gun. The cabin floor was typically stacked with ammo boxes. Later, the Cobra helicopter began replacing the Huey gunship with the same armament plus an automatic grenade launcher in the nose.

Finally, we used the Chinook CH-47 helicopter. They were capable of carrying an entire platoon. We did not like flying on them; they were not as agile as were the Hueys; it took them longer to land and take off. They were easier targets for the enemy than were the Hueys.

We were heavy cargo. Typically, with gear, we weighted 200 to 300 pounds each. Our suspendered harnesses and utility belts were laden with grenades, canteens, and ammo pouches. On some of our backs were frame packs strapped full of ammo and on others a PRC-25 radio with heavy extra batteries. Some men also carried 200-round cans of machine gun ammo. Around some were bandoleers full of extra loaded 20-round rifle magazines and all our trousers' kangaroo pockets were full of C-rations and that wonderful luxury, bug juice (insect repellant). These supplies made us large at the girth. There were no seats on a Huey. Holding weapons, rounds chambered but safety on, five of us hung on to the rising falling twisting turning helicopter with nothing but the cheeks of our butts and our feet.

A dike-top one-lane dirt road provided the only vehicular access to our village. That also served as our helicopter-landing pad. Split evenly on both sides of that road and down close to the ground, we would lay ready. Four to eight Hueys would suddenly land; we would be on them and in the air within seconds. The noise in a helicopter was too loud for any conversation, so once near the target area, the Lieutenant would signal for us to get ready. We would slip to the edge of the doors with our feet on the helicopter's skids ready to jump. When the helicopter was almost on the ground, the pilot would bring it to a sudden, split-second, hovering stop and the Lieutenant would give us a thumbs-down signal. We jumped immediately. Our last act just as we were jumping would be looking for something like a tree or a house directly in front of the helicopter's nose and at the compass in the center of the windshield. That was so we could orient our maps immediately after we were on the ground and know where to go. Even amid incoming enemy fire, one person would always orient a map in case we needed immediate artillery support. Note: the lack of a visible compass and an easy forward view was another reason we did not like the Chinook.

A day or two after our last ambush, a 3/4 ton truck along with several guards delivered a prisoner and an interpreter to the Old Man's tent. We had orders to go where the prisoner would take us. Vietnamese people were all well proportioned and slight of body; not this man. He was muscular, broad, and stocky. He could not be Vietnamese. Just as Caucasians vary from tall, light-skinned, blond, blue-eyed Scandinavians to shorter, olive-skinned, dark-eyed Mediterraneans to dark-skinned, black-haired Indians, so do Orientals vary. This man looked to be Mongolian. Even though a prisoner, he stood erect, proud, soldier-like, and impressive. He had to be regular army, not VC.

Three Chinook helicopters flew the company to an area west of our village. We landed in a clear area several hundred acres in size. It was obvious that this area was once rice paddies, for there were the remnants of dikes here and there. This large, clear area had a small river winding through it. The tide was going out as we began crossing the river. A few soldiers, but no machine guns, had already moved to the west bank of the river as the rest of us began to bunch-up at the river crossing. Suddenly we heard a large number of muffed thuds; 60-millimeter mortars rounds were headed our way. The rounds soon started landing in the middle of us that were on the east bank. Everybody hit the deck, hearts throbbing.

The sound of the mortars seemed to come from the edge of the jungle maybe 1,000 yards to our west. The enemy had to be where they could see us in order to shoot so accurately. We guessed at their location. In AIT, our DI told us about how they set up a 50-caliber machine gun for high-angle fire during the Korean War. They used a traverse and elevating tripod with the gun pointed at roughly a 45^0 angle to shoot over a mountain and heavily shower a road junction on the other side of the mountain. We needed to shoot our gun over our troops on the other side of the river. Many people think of a machine gun as a rapidly firing rifle. That is wrong. A machine gun is a shotgun, for the vibration of the gun as it fires and the variation in the ammunition shape a long narrow beaten zone. The further the bullets go, the larger the beaten zone.

I told Queen to use high-angle fire to rain bullets in the enemy's general area. We watched the tracers. Tracers burn out at about 1,000 yards so we could not follow the high-angle fire all the way down to the jungle's edge, but we could well guess where the rounds were landing. At this range, with high-angle fire, the bullets had to have a beaten zone two to three yards wide and forty to fifty yards long. Queen fired a six-round burst, and adjusted the angle of his fire a time or two until it was raining bullets on the edge of the jungle. He then moved his fire a little right and left thus spraying the area where we thought the mortars were. Quickly the other machine guns were doing the same thing.

Meanwhile, the mortar rounds were exploding within our ranks but exploding down in the mud. This was hair-raising. Flying, mucky mud landed on many of us, and a few GIs had shrapnel wounds, but the mortar fire killed no one. We were surprised at the number of duds that hit. The enemy simply had the wrong fuses for use in rice-paddy mud. Our machine gun fire must have frightened the VC, for after twenty to thirty mortar rounds, the enemy ceased fire.

In the confusion of the minute, the prisoner escaped. He was about to cross the river when the mortar rounds started landing. Evidently, when we hit the deck, he jumped in the river and rode the swift current away from us. No beginner, he knew exactly what to do and when.

Quickly after the mortar fire ceased, the CO had us finish crossing the river and form on-line;

meanwhile dust offs were evacuating our wounded. We moved out headed straight for the area from which the mortar fire came. Between the edge of the jungle and us, the river doubled back across our path and went into the jungle. We had gone maybe within 500 yards of the edge of the jungle and three women came out of the jungle poling in a sampan as fast as they could. The CO had the interpreter to scream out for the ladies to halt. The ladies kept on poling. The CO told us to shoot. Queen let loose a burst of six rounds and the lady in the middle of the boat fell into the boat. The ladies stopped but were not as fast to react as Banks, our head medic.

Banks was a conscientious objector and one fine soldier. He was the most skilled of the medics assigned to our company. As quickly as possible, he got to the ladies and was by himself with them several hundred yards from our main body. It takes guts to charge an enemy who is shooting at you when you can shoot back, but a conscientious objector has no gun and refuses to shoot back; that takes more guts. Banks was an easy target should the enemy have still been in place, but he went anyway. Banks was just plain brave. One bullet had gone completely through the lady. The CO immediately called for a dustoff for her while Banks stopped her bleeding.

We took up defensive positions as best we could in this clear area. None of us liked being out in the open. We were sitting targets with not so much as a dyke to get behind for protection. Meanwhile, the CO, through the interpreter, talked to the other two ladies. They were VC. By the time the interpreter was finished, the CO thought it useless to advance and saw no reason to hold the women based on what the interpreter told him. They were unarmed and likely not combat soldiers. They had accomplished their objective; they stopped our advance. They went on their way as soon as the Chinooks came to return us to our village.

The lessons of the day: Remember our training and past lessons; never go out in open areas; rather, go around the edge of open areas. Company-sized missions draw fire. Never bunch-up; that means stay two or three yards apart at all times. If you want to hand a guy something, move to him, give it to him, and then move away. We also learned some new lessons: We should always have a machine gun crew with the point squad. Further, those brave ladies had played us for fools. We should never have interrogated them but simply captured them and continued to keep pressing the enemy. While we forgot the basics, we also concluded that this mission came down from someone outside our unit; these were not the tactics of the 199th.

Company-size operations only occurred a few more times. Company-size movements were simply too easy for the enemy to see and too slow to move. That gave the enemy the opportunity to choose when and where to attack or to choose to avoid us altogether. The VC strategy: they were in this war for the long haul so pitch battle was not their intention, at least not yet. Staying alive and able to fight was their goal. Any opportunity to kill a few of us and run was a plus for them. With but a few exceptions, we now began what would be our routine until I left eight or nine months later: either we went on a local patrol by day looking for a place to set up an ambush for that night; or we went out on a platoon mission via helicopters or landing craft assault boats.

We did sometimes have interesting side trips. C-4 is a powerful explosive. It looks like gray modeling clay. You can use your hands to make it into any shape you wish just like with modeling clay. It is issued in gray blocks 11 x 2 x 1 1/2 inches that weigh 1 ¼ pounds. We had used it in training but had not used any in Vietnam yet. Today would be the day. We were to go into a defoliated area looking for VC rice. We were to find it and blow it up. Everyone but the squad leader carried a block of C-4, and he carried the caps and detonator.

Helicoptered to the area and dropped off in a small clearing, we set off with a compass expecting to find the rice. We went through an area where biting ants seemed to drop on us from the trees. Their bites were madding and left little red blisters. After having come out of that infested area, we soon found the rice. It was under a pole building – no walls, just a Mekong River Palm thatch roof. The pole building was maybe twenty by twenty feet with rice stacked eight or nine feet high – a lot of rice. We put caps into the blocks of C-4, wired the caps and located the blocks at intervals around the edge of the pile and forced them into it a foot or so. We moved away a safe distance, hooked the wires to the detonator, and then the squad leader set her off. The explosion was not only deafening, our heads felt like vibrating drum heads hit hard; the explosion literally rattled our brains. Rice dust drifted down for minutes. We went back to where the pole building had been. There was no rice, no building, just a shattered hard mud floor. C-4 is powerful. We maneuvered around the ant-infested area and caught helicopters out.

It takes shock to set off C-4. If you light it with a match, it will not explode but will rather burn with a hot-almost-invisible-blue flame. We had a block left over on purpose. You could roll a little C-4 into a ball the size of a green pea, stick that on the bottom of a can of C-rations, light it with a match and have a hot can of C-rations within half a minute. No GI worth his salt was going to pass up a luxury like that. That one block of C-4 lasted the squad for days.

Soon after that, with another reinforced squad, we moved along a series of dikes and through the rice paddies to northwest of our village and into a wooded area to see what was there. Not long after we entered the wooded area, we began following a path. Sergeant General Lewis, yes his first name was General, shouted, "Freeze!" We all did just as training had taught us and froze like statues. Sergeant Lewis then spoke, "Preston, your right leg is against a tripwire. Stay absolutely still." Lewis told the rest of us to move forty or fifty feet away. Lewis moved back and told Preston to walk backwards moving his left leg first. He did and all was okay. Lewis carefully looked and spotted a Russian grenade tied to a tree. Lewis moved back forty or fifty feet and shot the grenade. The bullet blew it apart, exploding the cap and causing a ball of fire. We had been through this exercise in training at Fort Benning, and we knew exactly what to do.

Booby traps were a favorite of the local VC and booby-trapped areas were nerve-racking. The VC had two ways of setting booby traps. One was what we had just seen; the VC would find two trees, one on either side of a trail. The trees might be big or small; however, our area's VC preferred smaller trees with small branches low to the ground to help hide the grenade. The VC would tie a Russian grenade to one of the trees somewhere between ankle high and knee high. They would tie a green trip wire to another tree three or four feet away on the other side of the trail. They then suspend the trip wire loosely between that tree and where it was tied to the grenade's pull-pin. They would camouflage the grenade by bending the small branches in front of the grenade. The green painted trip wire might be bare or surrounded by some refuse near the ground. Lastly, they would loosen the grenade pin.

The second way, used when they had captured American grenades, was also set between two trees as with the Russian grenades except they would put the grenade in an empty food can the right size to hold the grenade's dead-man switch (the spoon) in place. They then tied the can to a tree. Next, they tied the trip wire to the opposite tree and then tied the other end of the trip wire around the neck of the grenade. The VC would camouflage as before. Lastly, they pulled the grenade pin out with the food can continuing to hold the dead-man switch until some poor soldier had the misfortune to hit the trip wire pulling the grenade out of the can and in the direction of the soldier. I saw this same setup once where they had a grenade in a can on each end of one trip wire.

One note, training taught us that the enemy would use quick fuses in their booby traps so we expected booby traps to go off almost instantly. However, the VC we fought used Russian grenades with their standard three-second fuses for their loose-pin booby traps. The second kind of trap, the food can type, had our standard five-second fuses.

The Russian grenades were the kind used in WORLD WAR II. They were somewhat smaller than American WORLD WAR II grenades and not as smoothly cast. The firing mechanism was not inside the Russian grenades as were ours but stuck out of the top a couple of inches.

The true effect of booby traps was mostly psychological, for booby-trap fear did slow our movement in any area where hiding them was probable. In those places, we had to be super alert and move cautiously. Although finding booby traps in some areas was common, I only remember one man wounded by one. It was a staff sergeant who volunteered for some in-country training to do small unit reconnaissance patrols. He and three or four others would go out not to ambush but only to look and listen. On one of these patrols, he tripped a booby trap. He was badly hurt and, with no medic nearby, he lost his right leg and almost bled to death before he could get medical attention. Like most of our wounded, the Army never told us what happened to that staff sergeant. Not telling us what happened to our comrades in arms increased our apprehension; did he bleed to death or did he make it home? I thought then, and now, that not telling us was a mistake on the Army's part. They were our comrades in arms; we deserved to know what happened to them.

In training, our instructors taught us never to kick or turn over a dead enemy or pick up or move anything inside a house, around an enemy's campsites, or in an enemy bunker, for the VC could booby trap any item they thought a GI might disturb. That was counter to the request that we send anything we found of the enemy's back to the rear so that intelligence could evaluate what the enemy had or might be up to. We had been taking the risk of picking up such items and sending them back. However, one day we were back at battalion headquarters to catch some landing crafts assault boats, and some of our soldiers went into a little eatery / PX and saw a VC flag hanging on the wall and a Lieutenant carrying an AK-47. We had captured these things. After intelligence got through evaluating captured items, they were supposed to return them to us as war souvenirs. It was obvious that the GIs in the rear were confiscating them for themselves. Nothing else went back.

Above I said "local VC," for we fought the same group most of the time. We learned their tactics, and they seemed to have learned some of ours; therefore, we began changing things. After this booby trap incident, we would not walk on trails or on dikes but found it safer to wade through the rice paddies' mud no matter how deep and difficult.

Chapter 8: Things That Will Get You Killed

Going from civilian life to Army life was a huge change but a greater change was going to a life of nearly endless combat. Walking for hours upon hours in water-covered rice paddies where the mud was anywhere from two and three inches deep to up to the tops of our boots, and occasionally knee deep, all of us had "raisin" looking feet when we did get our boots off. Most of the tops of the raisin wrinkles had little puss pockets centered in small red sores – staph infection. They were about as much fun as the leeches we sometimes encountered. We lived with them both. Carrying heavy loads, rarely stopping, we lifted one boot and then the next as every mud-sucking step we took required effort. Laying down at night soaking wet, we rolled up in a poncho only to have body heat drive the moisture out, and we woke up dry for watch; that was our life. We could open and eat a can of C-rations while hauling a full load and stay on line while wading through a rice paddy. Eating three boxes of C-Rations, 3,600 calories, we burnt it all up and had no fat left on our bodies; we were nothing but muscles and bones. No longer did we carry anything but absolute essentials: weapons, ammo, grenades (exploding and smoke), water, food, and a small plastic squeeze bottle of bug juice. I would have given you a dime to carry a quarter for me if I had had a quarter, for the only money we had was "funny money," military scrip, and it stayed back in a little covey hole of our platoon's one big tent. We had nothing personal.

Gone were entrenching tools, bayonets, gas masks, etcetera. Being light infantry, we did not wear flak jackets like regular infantry. If we did not need it to survive, it was gone. No matter the circumstance, we could either make do or improvise all of our needs. We wasted nothing; even the cardboard box that our Cs came in was burnt up heating our instant coffee or instant cocoa. The M-16 flash-suppressor worked well when we needed to break the steel bands around a case of Cs. There was no television or movies; we learned the art of conversation.

Combat engineers provided our first luxury: showers beside the one-lane dirt road that went through the village. Oh, they were nothing like the showers we had back home. They consisted of a slat floor to keep our feet above the mud. They had one foot of open space at the bottom revealing feet and lower legs followed up by four-foot high sides to hide our private parts. Suspended a few feet above that, 2 x 8s held two fifty-five gallon drums. On the one side of the shower was a strong ladder going up to the drums. The drums had many small holes in their bottoms. One guy would carry a five-gallon jerry can of water up the ladder and pour maybe one and half gallons in one of the fifty-five gallon drums while the guy underneath wet up and then soaped up. Then the man on the ladder poured the other three and a half gallons, the rinse water. You dried off and put on shorts only to be soaked with sweat by the time you carried water up for your buddy. However, our greatest luxury was dry toilet paper. The Army had the white easy-to-see toilet paper concealed in a dull brown paper wrapper. We carried that on our elastic helmet band. Yes, we were now combat soldiers.

About the same time that we got the showers, one of our men had gotten a battery-powered civilian radio. Every morning he had it turned up so that all near our platoon's headquarters tent could hear it. Someone would rush to turn that radio down just before we heard the words, "Good Morning Vietnam!" It was a bit of a joke for we loved Armed Forces Radio and this early morning show was a great morale booster. Not only was it a way to hear a little about the outside world, the music was great and the humor was often. The letters from home, *The Stars and Stripes*, and Armed Forces Radio were that little bit of American culture that kept us going. The local Vietnamese also enjoyed listening to our music.

We still had much to learn about Vietnam. One day while walking down a dike just outside our village, I learned that there was more to fear in Vietnam than combat. I came across a fat, dark-gray-colored snake that was two-and-a-half to three-feet long. It was just lying still enjoying the sunshine. I had no idea what kind it was. I decided the best thing I could do was to disturb it so that it would move off the dike and I could get by. I picked up a palm branch, reached it out and lightly brushed the snake. It did not like that. It suddenly rose up on its rump and spread its head, obviously preparing to strike. It was a cobra. I did not know that cobras' heads did not fan out while they were crawling or just lying undisturbed. I did not know that, unlike our American snakes that just taper off to form a tail, cobras actually have a butt with a small tail extending from it. I was thankful that cobras do not strike at a high speed as do copperheads and rattlesnakes. It struck but I was too far back by then for it to make contact. I pulled out my forty-five and shot seven times, completely missing the snake. It crawled on and off with some speed. I told the local GI on perimeter guard what had happened and he radioed that it was just a snake. I then went immediately to the supply sergeant and got several boxes of 45-caliber ammunition and a bag full of the sergeant's empty beer cans. I then went to the bridge that split our village in two. The bridge was where we regularly did shooting practice. By late that afternoon, I was a far better shot with a forty-five. Lesson learned: I know the snakes of North Carolina but I best leave Vietnamese snakes alone.

Sometime after that Tet, the Lunar New Year, celebration came and we had a cease-fire agreement with the VC. We had placed our machine gun in front of a corner village house that gave us a 270-degree view of the rice paddies surrounding the town; that was just in case the cease-fire did not hold. The people in the house immediately to our rear motioned for me to join them for their celebration. I did. We all sat on the hard packed dirt floor around a large circular table with short legs. In its center was a big Lazy Susan. On the Lazy Susan were ten or twelve bowls of small pieces of different kinds of meats, small pieces of fish, shrimp, and relishes. The Vietnamese did not use knives and forks, only chopsticks; therefore, they cut meats, fish, and vegetables a size perfect to eat with chopsticks. The man of the house poured each man at the table a shot of rice whiskey. I do not drink whiskey. I spoke no Vietnamese and they spoke no English so I said no thank you as politely as I knew how to gesture with hands signals and facial expressions, but he insisted. They cooked their rice to a gummy consistency so it too was easy to eat with chopsticks. The lady of the house gave each of us a large bowl of that gummy rice. They each took a little of this and that out of the bowls on the Lazy Susan and placed the tidbits on their rice. I followed suit. As we ate, I recognized most of what I was eating, but one particular greasy meat had a strange taste. I motioned, "What is this?" They replied by holding their hands a foot and a half off the ground and said, "Bow Wow." I had just eaten dog. I quickly took that drink of rice whiskey. It was certainly strong enough to kill germs. Lesson learned: the Vietnamese would eat virtually any kind of meat.

One night, Sergeant Woollard had me go out as assistant to the other machine gunner in the weapons squad. Sorry, I do not remember his name but, like me, he had studied in engineering school, but his time in the service was soon to be over and Woollard thought that I might be the person to replace him. We went out and set up an ambush along a creek about half a mile from the village. It was a black night. We thought something was moving down the creek. Nothing was supposed to move along the waterways after sunset. The gunner asked me to fire a few rounds in the direction of the movement. The gun fired but only one round. I had been the one that cleaned our team's gun and that had been without a problem. I had cleaned this gun but put the gas piston in backwards.

I had the machine gun utility tool in my pocket and was able, in the dark, to unbolt the end of the gas cylinder chamber and reverse the piston. It was an embarrassing mistake; more importantly, it could have cost lives. I never made that mistake again. My teacher laughed and said that he knew the problem immediately, for he had done the same thing. The next day, I spent several hours with him. He knew much and I learned. We became friends, but before he left Vietnam, Queen lost an eye. I took over Queen's job. My friend's former assistant took over his gun. PFC Gardner became my assistant. He and I worked every minute we were in our village on doing our jobs smoothly. All of this went automatically for we were combat soldiers.

We often discussed ways to do things better. That could occasionally lead to failure and even death. Some idiot got the idea that we should use an inflatable boat, like those thrown off sinking ships for survivors, as a way to get to ambush sites. Sampans were extremely maneuverable. Over the centuries, sampans evolved as an ideal craft for these rivers and creeks with their heavy tidal flow. However, even a sampan is a sitting duck for any alert VC, but a life raft for a squad of heavy-laden soldiers – I know of nothing slower or harder to maneuver than a life raft yet, someone had the idea they would beat humping through the mud to an ambush site. The 1st platoon got the honors of testing this idea.

We were in our village the first and only evening a squad went paddling out in their life raft. We knew the sound of every kind of weapon. Suddenly, in the distance, we heard VC AK-47s and Russian Nagant carbines, but only one short M-16 burst. We quickly gathered around the Lieutenant's PRC-25. Nothing. Then we heard the 1st platoon leader radio that squad several times but with no reply. Thirty minutes to an hour later, that squad leader came walking in wet, muddy, alone, no helmet, and no weapon. Some minutes later, two more of his squad showed up wet, muddy, no helmets, no weapons. No one else came in. It was a disaster. In addition, we were all hurt and horribly disappointed at the squad leader's decision to run. We understood that his squad was overwhelmed, that he had lost his weapon and had to run out of harm's way, but, as a soldier, he had an obligation to stop running as soon as it was safe and observe. Were all of his men killed, were they wounded, were they captured? Why had he not waited hoping for other possible survivors? What could their platoon leader tell the families of those who lost their loved ones? It was painful for the entire company.

We were able to learn where it had happened. We had scouted the place several times. Lieutenant

Betz and those of us that were in that night began talking. When the VC had a success, they always repeated it. The CO will take a large contingent out to investigate at first light. Why not send out a reinforced squad in normal formation by an alternative route to meet the CO's investigation crew. Then five of us will hide in the bush where the VC got our boys. Our squad will then return at the same time as the CO's contingent but by a different route more spread out than normal. There will be so many of us coming in from two different directions, the local spies may well miss the five of us hiding. That is what we did.

After the two groups had met and had done our investigation, all ate our Cs while the five of us hid in a grove of trees near the river. My assistant and ammo bearer returned to the village. After sunset but before dark, we moved to the Mekong River Palms on the riverbank only to see a VC standing with his Kalashnikov. He was across the river approximately 200 yards away. He was watching the river. He had on the traditional dress of all of the farmers, black silk pajamas, but with a red and white stripe running up and down his pants' legs, no hat or helmet. We had never seen anyone have a stripe on the leg of his or her pants. We assumed it must be some part of the uniform of an officer or NCO. We knew that directly beside our opponent was a creek bed with the tide out. Our opponent's soldiers were likely heads down hidden on that creek's banks.

The quick plan: First Egan would call the artillery for VT (vertical timing) fire directly over the man, the creek, and hopefully his soldiers. Egan would have the artillery radio back just before they were ready to fire their artillery. Then Egan would take out the man with the striped pants. That would likely make his people expose themselves. The three others would take out targets of opportunity and I would fire, suppressing fire just before the exploding artillery arrived forcing the enemy to hit the deck and giving our exploding artillery the maximum number of prone enemies. Keeping the enemy in the prone position would increase the chance of achieving the direct hits when vertical-timed rounds explode; they are like giant shotguns raining down many pieces of high-speed shrapnel. It would be devastating.

That is what we did. Egan radioed the artillery. Egan fired at his target as VT left its guns. Egan's man collapsed in place. However, no enemy exposed himself or herself. I fired the suppressing fire just before the VT arrived. Vertical-timed 105 howitzer rounds explode sixty to a hundred feet above the ground sending shrapnel down and creating a larger kill zone. We had the artillery fire several volleys. Darkness came; we asked for flares. We saw no movement in the battled area. It was a long, tense night.

The next morning, soon after first light, the CO arrived with his usual numbers. They looked over the area. The night's tide had erased whatever happened in the creek bed and where there should have been the body of Egan's victim, there was nothing. The water had completely erased all but a few of the larger shrapnel holes. We five very tired men did not know if we had any success other than shooting the VC leader. We never found his body. That's combat.

While you never learn enough, we were making fewer and fewer blunders but still sometimes made foolish mistakes. For example, the platoon sergeant assigned our gun crew to Hathaway's squad for a routine daily patrol with the goal of setting up a nightly ambush along a distant creek. We had hiked a couple miles when the VC ambushed us. The enemy was obviously in strength and close. They pinned us down in a creek bed. We knew we were in trouble. Hathaway had no choice but to call in HE (high explosive) artillery. We were all down as the artillery was about to land, that is all but Hathaway. He decided to raise his head to see where the artillery was hitting. A large piece of shrapnel hit him just below his left eye. Hathaway's blood flowed as the artillery broke the enemy who disappeared. We called in a dustoff. Thank God that the shrapnel had lost much of its velocity before striking Hathaway. He wrenched the shrapnel out. We pulled out his first-aid packet, tied it in place and applied pressure. Hathaway was one of our best leaders, but in combat, even the best make mistakes.

Soon after this, we drew an unusual assignment, not in the rice paddies but in grassland mixed with spots of hardwood growth. Lenney's squad was to join a company of regular infantry.

Gardner, Newman, and I were to accompany them. The ten or twelve of us were to stay a 1,000 yards out in front of that company and run point for them. These soldiers had on flak jackets and their M-60 crews carried tripods. In short, they were so heavily loaded that we did not know how they carried all of that crap. That stuff was great for fixed positions but they probably could have gotten along better without the extras in these boondocks. We were darn glad that we were light infantry.

Lenney talked with their captain, established radio frequencies, and showed us on the map where we were to go. We then moved out in our usual slow, careful, quiet manner. At 1,000 yards out, we radioed them and then they began to follow us.

The day was uneventful and late in the evening the captain radioed and asked if we would like to stay in their encampment. We agreed. Once back, the captain said that he appreciated us blazing the way. He said that we could stay in the middle of the company's position, a large circle, and get some sleep. We thought that we were in for a good night's sleep, but these guys used something they called "recon-by-fire." They shoot something on and off all night. Our squad knew that if the enemy was in the area, they probably had two or three men carefully circling this company counting men, armament, and locations. All the enemy would have to do was decide whether to fight or flee. The VC did not like all out battles with large groups. In a case like this, normally the VC would fire 60 mm mortars and be gone before the rounds landed. We were more than a little nervous. Our squad did not sleep.

At first light, we were happy to move out to our 1,000-yard mark and begin our job of running point That evening, the captain radioed and offered for us to join them. However, not long before the captain radioed, we had found a good place for an ambush set-up. Lenney told the captain that we appreciated the offer but we felt more comfortable being his eyes all night, "just do not shoot in our direction." We felt much safer knowing that any local VC probably did not know where we were and were likely paying attention to where that company was. Located in a good position, we slept much better that night in the dead quiet that our usual sleep shifts provided. We began to feel that the tactics of the 199th were certainly superior to the tactics we were seeing. Recon-by-fire was more than a waste of ammo; it was simply a stupid tactic to use against VC. It gave the VC all the information they needed to plan a successful trap.

Chapter 9: We See Evil

The CO told us we had another company-size mission. On an island in the middle of the Mekong River, the VC confronted a political leader demanding that he help enlist soldiers to their cause. He refused. The VC then tied him up, cut off his eyelids so that he had to watch as the VC raped his wife to death. He still refused to help so they raped first his oldest daughter and then the youngest. Within days the women died, for there were no doctors in the Delta; the VC had killed or run off all professionals. The VC released the father to shame. He found his way to someone in our Army and asked that we go to that island and root the VC out. The CO said that we had to show our total support for leaders like this man and against the cruelty of the VC.

The next morning the entire company left after first light. Chinooks landed our three platoons in three locations at one end of the island. We then spread out from the landing sites making one line with roughly ten yards between soldiers. Our line stretched from one shore of the island to the other. Over a long day, we swept the entire length of the island ending up on the other end of the island looking at the South China Sea. We found no VC or signs of VC camps. However, some of our people did encounter the leader and he thanked us for coming so soon and showing support. Our people that met him said that he had indeed had his eyelids cut off and was obviously tortured beyond that. As was normal, at mission end, we formed up in defensive positions to wait on the helicopters to arrive.

While we waited on the helicopters, we saw how the crystal-clear the South China Sea was. We could see the bottom, undersea plants and fish swimming. Some of us laid down our gear in position and jumped in. It had been a lengthy, hot day and the water felt wonderful. We were diving and looking with amazement at the fish and plants. We also saw some green-colored snakes with finned tails in the water. About that time Banks, our head medic, came running screaming for us to get out immediately. He told us those pretty green snakes were sea snakes and were deadly poisonous. If one had bitten us, he could have done nothing but watch us die. So much for relaxing.

Once back in our village, that man and his dead family were on our minds. There were discussions of the wanton brutality of the VC. A discussion went on between Newman and me for several days. Torture is simply wrong. I remembered how my AIT drill instructor had told of such things. He had fought in WORLD WAR II, Korea, and Vietnam. He had related to us how, in WORLD WAR II, the Japanese indoctrinated its infantry in systematic cruelty. The climax of their training was bayoneting a Chinese prisoner to death. Plenty of whiskey, great fanfare and laughter accompanied this. Then, the graduate trainees had captured Korean women prostitutes for the night. The Japanese wanted to train their infantry that killing is fun. Forcing women into prostitution was but one of the Japanese abominations for which they have never apologized. Worship of the Emperor would ultimately foster atrocities ranging from death marches of captured allies to Kamikaze attacks on our ships and soldiers. Our DI said, "You will never act that way even in response to the worst things you encounter. You are American soldiers."   A machine gun crew is composed of a gunner who is the crew leader and responsible to pick the targets, range them, and engage them. The assistant gunner is responsible to keep ammo belted up to the machine gun as it fires and to call the shots telling the gunner where his fire is going and how much to adjust it: "Drop your aim six inches and fire." "Enemy moving up at three o'clock, fifty yards out." The ammo bearer not only carries machine gun ammo, he is responsible to distribute ammo cans throughout the squad and retrieve them to the assistant gunner as needed. The ammo bearer also carries a rifle and is responsible to watch the crew's flanks and rear. It is a team.

The raping to death of the three women became central to Newman's thinking after this island mission; he decided that the least he could do for that man, his wife and daughters was to keep up with how many VC he killed and notch his rifle butt. We decided that he had earned a third of the total kills of the crew plus the kills he had scored himself; he was a darn good shot and a fine soldier. If I remember correctly, at that time, he had two kills of his own with his rifle. I was not crazy about notching a gunstock, but I owed it to Newman to help make as good a guess as we could; we had been on the same crew since Fort Benning. Over the next few days, we discussed all of our engagements from the fifth night in country until now. We estimated how many we had shot and how many of those we killed versus just wounded. Newman wanted only kills on his stock. Given that most of our fighting was done at night, and the VC were as determined as we were to retrieve their dead and wounded, it became a pure speculation, but we finally decided that eight notches was as close to being accurate as possible. Over the months, Newman added more notches.

One of the career Army officers who taught ROTC at North Carolina State University said that the reason the military wants young men is that they have not learned to fear. That may be true, but exposure to enemy cruelty enhances caution and increases determination. America's best and brightest honor ethical conduct even when faced with fearful sites. You can look at war as black versus white; that makes it a game of live or die. That is easy: you did what you had to do to live, that makes it right; or you die, that is wrong; no moral component. Black versus white just does not balance. If you are trying to be civil, it is far more complex than that. I am not talking about chivalry. I am talking about what is just in war. After this mission, the war became more than North Vietnam conquering South Vietnam for its rich rice-producing land. It became about trying to protect another mother and two daughters. It became trying to prevent another father from being tortured in the worst possible way. Our war became about trying to prevent wrong, to prevent evil people's inhumanity. The father committed suicide a few days after we visited his island.

Chapter 10: 36 Hours

Hathaway was back! He had a huge scar under his left eye that covered much of his left cheek. It looked like a five-pointed star with jagged edges all around its points. The center was sunken in close to his facial bone. If this big Hawaiian did not already look tough, now he looked fearsome, and he was. He brought with him a case that contained a Starlight Scope. We had never heard of one. It was about two feet long and roughly three inches in diameter. It weighed five or six pounds. Hathaway was excited and said that it magnified starlight so that we could see out fifty or sixty yards at night. However, with no starlight or moonlight, it would not work. Soon after dark, we began playing with it. Every man who was going out the following night used it until he felt comfortable with it. Its picture was in black and green and revealed less detail than did the black and white televisions of the time, but there was no doubt that it would be an advantage over the VC's infrared equipment. While it was too heavy and bulky to mount on any of our weapons, it would allow the person on guard to spot danger at night.

After weeks operating out of our village, we had developed a routine designed to give us a little rest. We had three rifle squads and sent out one rifle squad one night and two the next night. However, since there were only two machine guns in a platoon, we machine gun teams often had to go out back-to-back nights. My team had been out the last two nights; however, the morning after we had learned to use the Starlight Scope, the Lieutenant assigned our crew to Hathaway's squad. In addition to his regular load, he carried that heavy Starlight Scope with its case strap slung over his shoulder. We were expecting to go out that night, set up and handle whatever came across our ambush, and return the next morning for another night in our village. It did not turn out that way.

We went out farther south of our village than we had in any recent patrols. Instead of walking around the edges of the rice paddies more or less concealed in the Mekong Palms, the harvest was in and the rice paddies dry; walking on a clear, dry rice paddy was easy. There was a house maybe a hundred yards to our front. Suddenly, an AK-47 shot a full magazine, fanning bullets across our line. The burst threw up a lot of dirt but hit no one. We figured that we had caught VC off guard, and that burst was to hit one or two of us slowing us down. That would give the VC a chance to skedaddle. Hathaway had no choice. He shouted, "Charge the house!" We had trained how to conduct classic infantry assaults in AIT, but this was the first such assault we had made in combat. It was frightening.

When a trained combat soldier hears that first burst of an enemy's guns, all of his training and experience take over for the first few seconds. Within those few seconds, the soldier gets hyper-alert and totally controlled by logic, no emotion (after it's over, you may come apart). Concentration is completely on what is happening. We ran like the wind toward the house and its connecting dikes. The shooter had to be in or to the right and behind the house. However, at the house, we could not find even a spent shell. The burst had to have come from somewhere behind the house or from under a large sheet of steel lying just to the side of the house. We chose not to shoot up the metal plate; we feared that a family might have taken cover under it. The VC would have loved nothing better than for us to kill some of the locals. We were American soldiers and absolutely did not want to hurt any civilians. Further, the steel sheet may have been booby-trapped with the hope that we would move it or shoot it.

We moved out quickly because we still felt like the VC's primary objective was to slow us down. Therefore, our best chance was to keep pressure on them by moving rapidly in the direction from which the twenty-round burst may have come. We had been only a hundred yards or so when another twenty-round burst fanned across our front. An AK-47 is not a long-range weapon; about 300 yards is its maximum effective range. Both poorly-aimed bursts definitely had to have come from that growth now about 200 yards to our front. We charged again. This kind of cat and mouse game continued off and on throughout the day. We moved fast enough to heap fear on the VC. After all, they had frightened the devil out of us. It worked, for the VC were never able to set up and even wound any of us, nor were we able to pin them down so that we could call artillery or gunships.

About dark, we arrived at a river junction and an abandoned triangular mud fort. The fort was maybe 50 feet by 50 feet by 50 feet. No one occupied the fort, so we checked it for booby traps. One corner was booby-trapped as were two sides of the fort. The booby traps were simply hand grenades with the pins loosened and hooked to trip lines only a couple of inches off the ground. We had no intentions of even trying to disarm booby traps – that will get you killed. We decided to stay in that fort for the night and occupied two corners and one wall. We figured that if attacked, the VC knew where the booby traps were and so would likely not attack from those directions, but we also knew that they could come from those directions and use the wall as their defense while they shot us. However, we felt that the VC's most likely tactic would be to slip up on the wall we occupied and throw a bunch of grenades in the fort, we gambled on the latter.

The walls around the fort were about four feet high, maybe four feet thick at their base, and maybe two feet thick at the wall tops. The walls would certainly stop any small arms fire but would be a liability against hand grenades thrown inside of the wall. We sat our machine gun up in the center of the cleared wall and checked each of the two corners so we could get our gun to either of them should the need arise.

We always carried more ammo than we felt like we might need. We moved all the squad carrier ammo to Gardner. Newman held his two cans in case something happened like a hand-grenade hitting the ammo Gardner had. Hathaway set up to Gardner's left. We choked down some C-rations and drank coffee before it was completely dark. We knew it was to be a long, scary night.

There was enough moon and starlight for the Starlight Scope to work but there were also some passing clouds now and then; those did cause viewing problems. About two hours after darkness, Hathaway said he saw someone crouched over, slowly walking toward us. Seconds later he said, "It looks like maybe a dozen spread out thirty to forty yards out to our front." Soon they would be close enough to throw hand grenades. I could not see anyone or detect movement. Hathaway moved just behind me looking over my gun. He slowly moved my aim to where he wanted me to fire. I let loose a burst of six rounds. He could easily see my tracer and the target in the Starlight Scope. He corrected my aim. I fired again and Hathaway said, "It looks as if you were dead on him." The enemy said nothing but all did go down on their bellies and began to crawl toward us. I expect it was first out of fear of the machine gun, but later, as we kept hitting them, they began to realize that they were taking casualties. They began withdrawing. Hathaway kept me moving aim from the closest man to the next until they moved out of the sight range of the Starlight Scope. Our fear was realized: our plan was correct. They planned to get within a few feet and throw grenades over the fort's wall directly on us. A half a dozen grenades would be devastating. They would then run away, proud of what they had done.

After maybe an hour, they were crawling again, this time to pull their wounded and dead away. Hathaway and I began shooting again. Gardner kept the ammo coming while Newman did what he could with little light to watch the back walls. The rest of the squad fired in the direction of my tracers. There were obviously more than a dozen of the enemy. They may not have known how we were doing what we were doing, however, the sky clouded over and we began to use only our ears. Through the night, we did have other times when Hathaway could see. They evacuated their dead and wounded but we did not have another attack until well after midnight. Then the light was enough for us to hurt them again. They retreated again. After that, things broke off just as the clouds returned. It was a long, long night.

As daylight came, so did reinforcements and a resupply of ammo, C-rations, and water. We were all party to the conversation between Hathaway, Lieutenant Betz, and our CO. With no villages around, the VC were too big a group to break up and blend in with other Vietnamese. Having casualties, they would be moving slower and have less time to find a place to set an ambush. The decision was that we would continue keeping the pressure on them by moving rapidly in the direction that the enemy had been heading the day before. Hathaway's squad and our gun crew would run point and push hard as we had the day before. We took off. We moved at a good pace through rice paddies and over creeks, but were still on line with other men from our platoon and other platoons to our flanks. By late afternoon we were suddenly in wet rice paddies. This slowed our pace considerably. We were approaching a large river.

Then about 300 yards from the growth along a river, the VC opened up with all they had. They made a similar mistake to yesterday's mistakes when they failed to take careful aim before firing; they should have waited until we were closer. Most VC would have been better at taking aim and certainly would not have fired until we were close. This had to be another unit and not the enemy we had been fighting for weeks. The bullets hit no one but only kicked up mud on us.

It sounds strange, but we were so tired that all of the adrenalin in the world could not make us move but so fast. Two of our boys made it to cover behind a cemetery's edge and turned parallel to it, laying as flat on the mud as they could. The cemetery was like everything else in the Delta, a built-up area maybe four or five inches above the rice paddy. The cemetery was rectangular with one edge along the river. Gardner and I moved into the cemetery to our buddies' flank. Dotted with tombstones and vaults, it provided some cover against direct fire. Newman was not far off. Someone of the enemy knew Gardner's and my location and kept bullets ricocheting off the gravestones. The VC had our squad pinned down and unable to return effective fire.

I do not know what was happening on our flanks but some fine soul called the gunships. I could see our two boys pinned down behind the cemetery's edge. There were some watermelons growing on the edge of the cemetery, and they had somehow gotten one of the melons. Unable to fight, they had broken it open and were eating while flat on their stomachs. The lead gunship came in close and let loose rockets over their heads. Hathaway's radioman was close enough that I could hear the pilot ask if he had gotten too close to our boys behind the cemetery. "No, they are okay. Thank you!" Evidently, the VC had been fighting a delaying action so that their main body could cross the river, for those rockets ended the incoming fire. Crossing the river this late in the day with the VC likely set up on the other side was too dangerous. The gunships could take over for now. After a head count, the transport helicopters came and picked us up.

We were exhausted. I barely got into our village, and I laid down in a grassy side ditch to rest. I woke up hours later smelling some disgusting odor; I had been so tired that I had laid down and slept in hog shit.

Chapter 11: Officers from Excellent to Disgusting

It was a bit unusual for Lieutenant Betz to join us on what was a routine squad-sized ambush, but there he was. I did not know that he would soon be leaving us; in retrospect, I believe that he must have just wanted to spend another night or two in the bush with us before going home. We set up our ambush on a site where a home used to be. The growth around the home's old dirt floor provided excellent concealment. The night was uneventful. Soon after first light, we had eaten our Cs and were ready to move out when someone spotted three armed VC in the distance. The only weapon that had a chance of engaging the VC was my gun. Betz asked me if I could get them. They were 1,100 yards out and walking on a dike toward an area of thick growth. I laid down in the prone position with bipods extended and attempted to target them. At that range, with my eye but six or eight inches off the ground, I could not see them. I stood up and saw that they would walk in front of a coconut palm in just a few more yards. I told Gardner to tell me when the first man was three yards from the palm tree. I lay back down with my sights set on 1,100, maximum effective range of the M-60, and aimed at the palm. In a few seconds Gardner said, "Hit it." I fired a bust of six and quickly he gave me a correction and I then shot several bursts of six, coming back on target after each. The VC had no warning; the noise of the first burst would have gotten to the VC about the time the second burst of bullets arrived. Gardner said, "They are down." We did not know if we hit any of them or they went down because the bullets came close. Betz was pleased and we moved out in the direction of several other squads who were in the area for what was to be a sweep. Betz went right by where the three went down and sent word up the line that all three were dead. I said to myself, "That was a lot of luck." I do not remember the rest of the day being eventful until we got back to our village: The CO was leaving and we would get a new CO.

The next day the new Captain arrived. I was among the few from each platoon stationed on our perimeter while the new CO had a company formation and gave a speech. After the speech, a sergeant was my relief. I asked him what the new CO had to say. He responded, "A bunch of shit. Don't worry about it." I left, headed for a local Vietnamese eatery. The eatery was on the other end of the village, so by the time I got there twenty to twenty-five GIs relieved from the perimeter were seated. I had no more than sat down and the 1st platoon sergeant came in, had us go outside, lined us up, and marched us back to the CO's tent. It was the first time we had marched in formation since getting on the ship before we left Okinawa. Once at the CO's tent, the platoon sergeant gave us parade rest and one by one took us in to see the new CO. He had told the formation that we were not to fraternize with the Vietnamese. When it was my time to go in, he asked me why I went straight to the eatery after he gave his talk. I explained that I was on the perimeter when he gave his speech, and when my relief came he said that there was nothing new said. The CO said, "That is no excuse." Why did he not have the courtesy to give us the speech? No. He busted all of us one stripe. We felt as if we were back in basic training and this CO was trying to send a message that he was tough. We were professional soldiers; war had made us much tougher than this officer could possibly imagine. We were also disappointed in the 1st platoon sergeant; he should have told us what was up but he did not.

At Fort Benning, and particularly on the ship, our trainers emphasized politeness and consideration toward the Vietnamese. These poor people were living in the middle of a war; the little money we spent at the eatery, having ladies wash our clothes, and so forth was a help to them. I do not know where this Captain came from but his first actions backfired on him. Betz made sure those in his platoon made rank back quickly, but we had a bitter taste in our mouths.

As best as I remember, the 199th had done such a good job that our General moved up in rank and on to the 4th Infantry Division. It was a very short time after this that all of the officers who had gone through training with us at Fort Benning rotated out. Lieutenant Betz said that he was going back to Idaho and farm potatoes. Our new platoon leader, a graduate of the ROTC program at Texas A&M, was personable but we were soon to learn that he was not ready for this assignment. He did grow but, like the other new platoon leaders, he did not understand what we were about. On his first day with our company, the new platoon leader of the 1st platoon actually had the two squads that were going out to stand inspection before they left. He chewed them out for looking so sloppy and made them go get their bayonets and several entrenching tools. Entrenching tools in rice paddies? How can you dig a foxhole in this mud? This group of officers simply did not have the training they needed, and none appeared to have combat experience.

At the entrance to our village, immediately after the new CO arrived, he ordered a bunker built. The previous CO felt that such positions were but targets. This new CO felt that it was necessary to control who came and went from our village. A few days later, I was on duty at the bunker when a helicopter landed and all of the new platoon leaders and the new CO got off. They had been to some sort of party and were clearly drunk. This is a combat zone and all of our officers were smashed; we were not accustomed to such dangerous nonsense. I came to attention, saluted, and greeted my platoon leader with, "What's happening!" He grabbed me by the collar and said, "What's happening!" as if I had said something that was disrespectful; that was certainly my intention. I answered, "Not much, sir!" He loosed his hold on me and went on his way never to mention the incident.

With the new officers came another change, we started operating a squad of us alongside a squad of Vietnamese Rangers. Unlike when the last CO was commanding, no one explained what the purpose of this was. However, in spite of the language barrier, we went on to learn things from the Rangers. We learned to snap the Mekong Palms' leaves in such a way that they broke quickly without the use of a knife or machete. They showed us how to quickly make a monsoon-proof shelter from the palms' branches and blend it in with the places we liked to hide during ambushes. The Rangers also taught us what wild plants were edible and how to tell when they were ripe. They taught us how to catch the crabs that lived in the rice paddies and how to cook then in a straw fire. We used grenades to fish. The shrapnel did not go far under the water, but the shock of the exploding grenade stunned the fish and they floated to the top of the water long enough for us to grab any that were big enough to cook. The Rangers taught us to boil the fish. The things the Rangers taught us gave us breaks from C-rations. However, years later, I found that I had likely caught liver flukes and that I had had typhoid fever. The doctor who found indications of liver flukes said that there was no way to tell where I had gotten them; however, they were present in the Delta. A year or two later, another doctor found that I also had had typhoid fever. This doctor was from Africa and familiar with the disease, he was a bit more positive about its origin.

The Rangers were good soldiers; however, armed with our WORLD WAR II weapons, they were at a disadvantage against the VC. Given the small stature of most Vietnamese, it was common to see a soldier who was not much taller than his M-1 or BAR (Browning Automatic Rifle) was long. The M-1 and BAR did have the advantage over the M-16 when it came to range and power, but their weight and the weight of 30.06 ammo made these weapons absolutely wrong for these small people. They preferred the M-1 carbine that was better suited to their size and its ammo was lighter.

As we were learning to work with these Rangers, the inexperience of our platoon leader gravely hurt the relationship with them. It was evening and our platoon had been working a sweep with a platoon of Rangers. A helicopter brought out a hot supper for the Rangers and us. That was an unusual treat. However, for some reason, our platoon leader saw some cause not share these rations with the Rangers. Indeed, he poured out the Rangers' portion as soon as we ate. They went to bed hungry. We were embarrassed and the Rangers were angry. I am sure the VC loved this inhospitality and probably used it as a recruiting tool. With a CO that did not like the Vietnamese and woefully inexperienced officers, for our company, the experiment in partnership with the Vietnamese Rangers was dead.

Our Platoon Leader had to go back to the 199th headquarters where evidently they all but busted him. He came back from the meeting far more humble than he had been. He had frightened us with his loud voice on the few ambushes in which he had participated. We would be ready to settle in for the night's ambush and he would act as if we were on break. He would start telling us about his adventures at Texas A&M in a voice that could be heard for miles. In the Delta, there was no electricity, hence, no background noise or background light. Even a cough could give you away and a lit cigarette was visible for a mile or more. After the butt chewing, the Lieutenant began to listen to us. He learned to whisper at night and talk only about things that were of immediate importance. He learned to speak only as loudly as was necessary when out during the day.

One morning not too long after that, another insane event happened. We had just gotten in from a bushwhack and were cleaning our weapons when a heavy concentration of tear gas rolled in. We knew of no incident where the VC had used gas, but here it was. When there was any threat to our village, we were immediately to go to our defensive positions around the village. We had gas masks in our platoon tent, but we did not go get them. We all knew that tear gas was uncomfortable but that we could operate in it when under attack and so we did. We got to our positions only to find out that the CO had set the tear gas off.

In a village of roughly 500 civilians, the new CO had set off tear gas to teach us to keep our gas masks near? All around the village women and children were screaming and the men crying. I particularly remember one lady who looked at me with tears pouring from her eyes and her poor sick child in her arms; her face said, "What is going on?" The villagers had no idea what tear gas was. When they found out that our CO had set it off, they were furious. So were we! We came to Vietnam to help these poor people and this idiot of an officer tear-gassed them. He had single-handedly ruined all of the effort spent building a good relationship with these people. He had become not only a recruiting tool for the VC, I am sure some locals were now happy to volunteer information to the VC – how many Americans left when, what equipment did they carry, and in which direction did they go. I do not think that our new officers understood the definition of "Search and Destroy," the mission of the 199th. Search and destroy meant to search out the enemy and attack him there. These officers seemed to think that it meant to burn the place down.

Next, I found out that the Captain had gotten several copies of *The Art of War* by Sun Tzu. I borrowed a copy and read it. It was a collection of axioms, advice for even the greenest private all the way up to the Commander in Chief. It was worth the read and study. However, when I was told that it was how we would be operating, I thought to myself, these officers should first read *Emily Post's Etiquette* and then *Mosby's War Reminiscences*.

We hit a hot LZ (landing zone) not too long after the tear gas event. That battle and some hard work by our first sergeant helped these officers act more appropriately in combat, but they were still woefully short of the skill level of the former CO or our Lieutenant Betz. They were full of self-importance. They never even attempted to repair the damage they had done to our relationship with the locals. Mosby was successful in large part because he had the support of the population.

Chapter 12: Replacements

These episodes with our new officers had an effect on us all. Lanny was a squad leader. We were assigned to be with his squad on a routine bushwhack. Nothing happened that day or night but the next morning, Lanny went crazy. We had set up by a creek but did not leave soon after first light as was usual. Instead, Lanny talked foolishly. He wanted to see how long he could hold a grenade before he had to throw it. He commenced to pull the pins, let the spoons fly, and hold the grenade while counting and then at the last instant throw the grenade into the creek. When he ran out of his grenades, we insisted that we get back to our village. Several of us talked to our platoon sergeant and Lanny was gone. He had been a squad leader since Fort Benning. It hurt to see him go, but it was obviously necessary.

We had not only lost our officers, we had lost strength due to casualties and the rotation of both enlisted men and NCO's. One at the time, we began getting replacements. The new enlisted men were green, but our new NCO's were of excellent caliber. Our new platoon sergeant was an ex-DI (Drill Instructor). He could be sympathetic, respectful, or tough, depending on a man's needs. He was perfect for us. PFC Locklear died within three weeks of his arrival. That hurt. Other replacements were wounded early on. We soon realized that our replacements were simply not as well trained as we had been when we arrived! Further, they had no fear, no understanding of just how dangerous combat is. We learned that the best first assignment for each of these replacements was as a radio operator at the squad level. That way they would be under the direct supervision of the squad leader and able to hear what was going on over the radio, able to hear our maneuvering, calling in artillery, helicopters, dustoffs, supplies and so forth. That worked well for us; it likely saved some lives.

A big problem for the new GIs was adapting to the climate, the time change, and simply not being strong enough to carry heavy loads for hours on end through rice paddies. Troop ships are notoriously slow. It had taken us close to a month to float over on the *USAT Sultan*. Although we did not like ship life, it had advantages: we were pretty well adapted to the climate and the time differential when we arrived in Vietnam. Our replacements had flown from somewhere in the States and thus immediately gone from a far more moderate climate to the Mekong Delta where it was ninety-five in the shade with very high humidity. They exited the airplane directly into a steam bath; sweat poured. Further, they had to endure a twelve-hour time difference; night was day and day was night. Add to that, we had been in excellent shape when we left Fort Benning; we were quickly able to adapt to carrying sixty to a hundred and twenty pounds through the mud-sucking rice paddies for hours on end. They just were not in excellent physical condition. More than one fell victim to heat exhaustion. Then there was the filth; we lived, ate, and slept in rice paddy mud where animal dung was the common fertilizer. Such was the place they had just arrived; it was shocking even to the strongest.

For example, we had gone on a patrol assigned to stay the night in a WORLD WAR II Japanese fort with some South Vietnamese soldiers. Late in the day, after finishing our day's patrol, we arrived at the fort. One officer was in charge; he greeted us with a happy smile. The VC had been attacking the fort; we were there to reinforce the garrison with its twenty-five to thirty soldiers. The fort was triangular. The outside length of the walls was eighty to maybe a hundred feet. They were roughly twenty-five feet high and twenty-five to thirty feet thick. The soldiers billeted in the interior of the walls. The small triangular courtyard at the fort's center was barely large enough to handle a tight formation of the few soldiers quartered there. They had no machine gun, not even a BAR. They just had M-1 Garands and M-2 carbines.

The officer offered to let everyone sleep inside the walls where his men stayed. All but Gardner and I chose to do so. We looked out of all of the rifle slots and old Japanese machine gun positions; none offered more than a narrow view of the surroundings. However, on top of the thick wall, Gardner and I could see for miles across the surrounding rice paddies and into the few distant areas of the thick growth scattered here and there. We could also relocate quickly and shoot in any direction. Even being but a few feet back from the outside edge of the wall was protection against any enemy flat trajectory fire. Our only fear would be mortar or artillery fire. The only such weapons the local VC had were 60 mm mortars. We felt like the top of that wall would be a great place from which to fight. We did locate near the staircase in case there were mortar fire. We slept on the wall. The night was uneventful.

We left after first light. Spec-4 Stringer was the first one to start itching. Soon all but Gardner and I were scratching. The rest of the squad had slept on lice-infested bedding. That was particularly tough on Private Tannelly, our latest replacement. He was carrying a twenty-six-pound PRC-25 radio, two six-pound extra batteries, his rifle, ammo, and all of the usual gear in the ankle deep mud of the rice paddy and the humid heat. He was from New York City and had never really been in any kind of good physical condition until he joined the army, but Basic Training and AIT were not enough to prepare him physically. On the way back to our village he said, "This place is pure hell!" We died laughing. Someone responded, "Don't talk so loud, Tannelly. Wait until you get in butt-deep mud, can hardly move and the VC starts shooting at you." However, the capper for Tannelly was when we got back to our village, he was totally exhausted. Our medic gave him a can of *Raid* insect killer and ordered him to get naked and spray every inch of his body, his clothing and his helmet, "Right now! before you do anything else. We don't want your disgusting crabs." *Raid* was the most effective and quickest treatment for body lice. Tannelly was one miserable human being. Such is always a time for humor. One of the guys said something like this, "Tannelly, what you need is a good ice-cold beer in one of those big frosty mugs." "Yes!" responded Tannelly. His antagonist answered, "If you can slip unnoticed down to the Vietnamese eatery – it's down the road about a quarter of a mile – they'll sell you a beer. Of course, it won't be cold but they can give you some ice to put in it. But, be careful about the ice, it usually gives you the squirts." The Lieutenant gave Tannelly his promotion to PFC a day or two later; however, I do not think that helped his mourning a bit. The funniest part, Tannelly said that he had joined the army to get away from his nagging wife.

A not so funny incident occurred on a new man's first mission. We were in company strength about to sweep through an empty village looking for anything that might help the enemy. We charged as we got close to the first row of houses. This just-off-an-airplane private ran to a window, threw a grenade through the window, stood with his back against the palm-thatched house, and got a back full of shrapnel. Luckily, he had thrown it too hard and it was against the rear wall of the house when it exploded, far enough away to pepper his back but not kill. His helmet protected his head. It never entered our minds that someone would not realize that grass houses do not stop shrapnel. Too much television, not enough training.

Another replacement was PFC Hatch. He was from California and did not realize the seriousness

of our business. Our new platoon sergeant gave him
to me as assistant gunner and moved Gardner to
another gun. The platoon sergeant wanted me to
train Hatch to be my replacement on our gun and for
me to become a squad leader. I started working with
Hatch on how to keep the gun in immaculate
condition; how important it was to keep the ammo
in its cans until ready to use, no bandoleers of
machine gun ammo that would get dirty and jam the
gun. He did not understand why he had to learn to
disassemble and reassemble the gun blindfolded, but
he did it. Then it was how to hit the dirt and open a
can and hook a new belt to the belt being fed into
the gun in seconds as Gardner did so well. I taught
him the lingo Gardner and I had developed when he
was calling my shots, adjusting my fire. Hatch was
flippant, but he got serious on our first mission
together.

We were part of a reinforced squad. We were
going through a village that appeared empty but had
found two VC and taken them prisoner. Moore,
along with the prisoners, ran point. The two
prisoners walked a few feet in front of Moore with
him pointing his rifle at them every step of the way.
Hatch and I were behind Moore maybe five yards.
Spread out in a line behind us were Newman,
Hathaway, and the rest of the squad. We walked on
through the village hoping to get to the other side so
we could call a helicopter to pick up the prisoners.
We came through some thick growth to a rice paddy
that was maybe fifty feet across and then into some
more growth on the other side. I told Hatch that we

would wait in this growth on the ready while Moore and his prisoners went across the dike and into the next growth. Moore was half-way over when a shot rang out. Moore was shot. He immediately hit the deck. So did the two prisoners. I opened up shooting over Moore and the prisoners, heavily spraying the growth in front of where they lay. I shouted for the medic and Hathaway. Hatch and I covered for Hathaway and the rest of the squad as they moved across the rice paddy quickly and into the growth. Newman covered our rear. One of the other men took the prisoners. The medic attended Moore. The bullet had gone through his elbow. Hatch and I, followed by Newman, then crossed over.

There was a lot of blood. We had obviously hit someone. Next, we went into the house that was just inside the growth and found a bunker inside. We threw grenades into the bunker. Hathaway called gunships, for a dustoff for Moore and for someone to pick up the prisoners. I told Hatch, if you had been the gunner and had been crossing behind Moore, that VC would have shot you. The VC had far rather shot a machine gunner than anyone else in a squad because, "As a gunner, you will have the overwhelming firepower that terrifies the enemy." The incident had frightened Hatch severely. He was finally serious about his job.

I took over Lanny's old squad. Newman was also given a squad. My first night out with my squad, our platoon leader sent us to patrol an area we had never been in before and had us set up on a river that was maybe a hundred yards wide. Setting up on a wide river was not normal; we preferred creeks ten or twelve yards wide so that we would be close to our targets when we opened up. During the night we saw what we thought was a sampan on the other side of the river. We opened up. I called for flares. The light arrived. We had killed a tree that was peacefully floating along near the bank on the other side of the river. No matter how long you are in combat, you continue to learn. This lesson: stick to narrow creeks where you can hear the enemy even if you cannot see them well.

Having been on a machine gun crew since Fort Benning, I had little experience shooting an M-16. As squad leader, that is what I carried. We trained on M-14s in Basic Training and AIT. The M-14 was a darn good rifle. I quickly learned that the M-16 was not. It had its advantages: It was light to carry, and one could carry three times the ammo. However, these first M-16s were not as accurate nor did they have the range of an M-14. Knowing how many times my machine gun was the only weapon that could reach out and touch the enemy, I felt that it would have been nice if one of my riflemen could carry an M-14. That was true for those more distant target opportunities, opportunities that particularly occurred when the weapons squad leader did not have a machine gun crew assigned to a squad.

Upon talking to one NCO with far more experience than me, all became clear. Soldiers fired approximately 1,000 rifle rounds for each enemy killed in WORLD WAR II and Korea. Further, most kills were made at less than a hundred yards. The M-16 did not have the range of the 03 Springfield or the M-1 or the M-14 but had the advantage of also being able to fire either semi or fully automatically. The Army wanted to increase the infantryman's ability to make kills at less than a hundred yards. The M-16 gave the infantryman the ability to carry more rounds and fire faster. That equaled more kills. I understand that the M-16s carried today are superior to the ones first used in Vietnam, but in the flat open rice paddies of the Mekong Delta, we also needed the range and power of an M-14.

Our previous CO had been correct; it was not too long before a sniper was shooting at the two men in that stupid bunker. Soon after that, the sniper took shots at our mail truck. The only road to our village was nothing but a dike one lane wide. Every afternoon a three-quarter-ton truck would drive down that road leading to our village. The truck brought the mail and other supplies. The truck, like the bunker, was an ideal target for a sniper.

We decided to do what had worked well before; a reinforced squad went out to search the area where the sniper was likely positioned. All of the villagers observing us would expect that. We all moved into the bush and did a thorough search. That thicket covered many acres and provided plenty cover for the VC to approach our village undetected as well as room for them to maneuver. We found a good position in the edge of the bush facing the road. It was likely the position the sniper had been using. I called in a few rounds of artillery to establish some barrages thinking we might need them in the coming night. VC informants trying to observe us from the village would have thought that we had found something. The soldiers who then went back to the village spread out and took their time going back to the village. Five of us hid, ate our C-rations and waited. Near dark, we moved near the edge of the bush into position with our backs to the road. That bit of bush was visible to our troops in our village; that meant that we only had to worry about what was in the thicket to our front.

Soon after dark, we heard something moving through the growth not far to our front. We then heard some soft talking. It had to be VC. The new man on the radio wanted to shoot. I quietly but firmly told him, "No." I decided to call in one of the barrages. I quietly whispered into the microphone something like, "Fire barrage red." In just a few minutes in came the rounds. It was then that we heard very distinctly the VC talking; obviously, someone was giving orders and not being quiet about it. That meant that he likely did not know those calling in fire on them were nearby. The talking also told us pretty much where they were. I did not want the artillery any closer to our position and so I asked for gunships to come in from the opposite direction. While they were coming, I had the "barrage red" fired again. The gunships arrived. We had the VC in a triangle. We were on one side and not too worried that the VC would try to escape in our direction and over a rice paddy in plain view of our fully alerted troops in the village. Artillery fire checked the second side of the triangle. Helicopters covered the third side. We heard gunship fire several times but did not know if they were successful, for I did not want to be on the radio for fear the VC might hear me giving away that we were near. While I was certainly a hardened soldier, such nights still frightened me; frankly, they seemed more tense than earlier in my tour.

I was just a Spec-4 squad leader. However, unbeknownst to me, the General had been listening in on our radio communications. He sent word that he wanted to meet the sergeant that ran that ambush. The CO promoted me to buck sergeant that morning just before the General came out to congratulate our squad.

My squad picked up another new man soon after that. He was a pugnacious wise guy from Chicago. He seemed to be street smart. I explained to him that many of these men were hardened soldiers, trained killers, and would not tolerate his loud arrogance. My words did not take. He remained loud and obnoxious. I knew that he was intelligent and could be an asset, but he would have to get the chip off his shoulder if he was going to be an effective soldier.

I decided the best thing to do was make him my squad's radio operator thus keeping him beside me at all times. In a few nights, we had to provide two men for that bunker at our village entrance. I decided that it would be Pugnacious and me. That night I took the time to tell him more of what we had learned, our procedures, and I explained the why of each. One of our procedures was to only whisper at night and to say only what was necessary. Another standard procedure was to wake sleeping soldiers by tapping them on their boots. We had all learned to wake immediately when we felt that tap on our boots. Anything else, he was to assume, was an enemy.

I had him take first watch. At the time for second watch to begin, I was sleeping, dead to the world, face down on a cot using my rifle as a pillow, and someone grabbed me by the back of my shirt and spoke loudly. In a split second, I had the man on the ground with my knees on his shoulders, one hand on his neck and the other hand in a tight fist ready to smash his skull in, it was "smart mouth." He had no idea how strong a professional soldier could be when he felt his life threatened. I said words to the effect, "Tough guy, there are thirty men in this platoon and every one of them could beat your butt in a New York minute. You can join us and maybe not get shot dead or blown up or worse, captured by the VC; then, just maybe, go home in one piece in thirteen more months. Or, I can ask the first sergeant to send you back to fill sandbags and guard an ammo depot. Do you understand?!" He whimpered, "Yes, sergeant." Even though I was a warrior, I hated violence as a motivator. However, he was a different man after that. Just before I left Vietnam, our platoon sergeant asked whom he should appoint as my replacement. I recommended that man. Without doubt, training our replacements was not only one of most challenging parts of being a soldier, it could be frightening.

Chapter 13: Time in Vietnam Grows Short

Many of our drafted soldiers' time in service
ended while in Vietnam. Thus, some NCOs and a
number of enlisted men had rotated out. However,
our company still had a core of the GIs who had left
Fort Benning and floated over on the *USAT Sultan*.
The core rotated out during the last three months in
Vietnam, roughly a third of us each month.
Newman and I were among the last third. We had
been through much together. That last month found
us tense, anxious, cautious.

On a routine search and destroy, we came
upon a little village having only five or six houses.
There were a large number of coconut palms in and
around palm-thatched homes. The sky was clear
blue; the tide in with the rice paddy water reflected
the scene: a scene for a picture postcard. Stopped
waiting on something, I do not remember what, I
was able to stare at the village for more than a few
minutes. Home came into my mind; would I be able
to get out of here in one piece or even get out of here
at all? I then remembered Craggy Gardens on the
Blue Ridge Parkway near Asheville. Why my mind
went there, I do not know; maybe it was because it
too was a beautiful, peaceful place. I wanted to see
it again. Would I?

For the third time since we were in the Delta,
there was a lull in the fighting. During these lulls,
the VC seemed to disappear for a week or three. We
had finally realized that the lulls occurred at rice
harvesting and planting times. The VC had to go

home and help their farmer families. These lulls always ended with a bang. Our stressed troops tended to get sloppy during these lulls. I could not let my squad's new people relax; I had to ready them.

On a machine gun crew, I had the opportunity to serve with each squad numerous times. Each squad leader was different: one was cautious, another sort of in the middle, and then there was Hathaway. Hathaway was by far the most aggressive. I used this lull as a chance to teach my squad that combat calls for total dedication of all of your mental and physical abilities. They must know that the end of the lull would come when least expected. It seemed my personal fears made me more assertive; it seemed the safest way to fight. While I planned to be as aggressive as Hathaway, with several new privates onboard, I saw that as an error – something for later, after my new men were better at soldiering. That turned out to be a good decision.

Our CO sent us on a reconnaissance patrol. Now, we were combat troops and not skilled in reconnaissance, why send us? I got my answer that night. The area we were to recon was along a large river; oceangoing ships were passing by. Lined up and down one bank of the river was an oil depot with its many huge tanks of petroleum products. A tanker was unloading. Directly across from the depot was a mangrove swamp. Mangrove trees only grow in tidal swamps. Exposed at low tide are the trees' roots, a tangled mess so dense that one cannot begin to go through them. We were to patrol the mangrove swamp within a three-mile radius of the oil depot.

It was afternoon and low tide when we landed maybe a mile north of the depot. The landing craft headed up a wide creek but was only able to go a few yards before she bottomed out. We got out of the landing craft and then waded maybe fifty yards in deep mud onto a small island where we could walk.

Once on the island, we moved with maps in hand so as not to get lost in the tangled mess of mangrove. We made our way several hundred yards in from the river and worked our way south parallel to it. We moved from one island through thick roots and mud and onto another island and then another. On the islands, the VC had cleared small areas, placed mortar-aiming stakes, and built the mud bunkers for artillery protection. It was plain to us, these VC were planning to either hit the petroleum depot, a ship traveling the river, or something larger. We marked the location of each island on our maps. We carefully moved some of the aim stakes enough to cause error and concealed the holes left by them by carefully tamping down the ground. Would it work, or would the VC catch the error? Who knows but we had to try.

Moving was slow and so, as the day ended, we had only gone maybe a mile down river from where we had landed. We stopped on one of the small swamp islands along a creek that was ten to twelve yards wide. It was plain to me that we had no need to worry about ambushing foot traffic or protecting against an assault by foot soldiers. If we saw anything that night, it would be on the creek. It was an excellent position being in a bit of a bend in the creek. That bend was such that we were able to see down the creek a hundred yards or more in each direction. Using the map and our radio, I worked with the artillery to set up barrages along the creek at a safe exploding distance from us. As it was getting dark, we settled down in the growth along the creek and ate our C-rations. Thank the LORD; it was a clear night with some moonlight.

High tide came some time after dark, and with it we saw a sampan coming up the creek. We had a new soldier carrying our squad's radio, "Sergeant, when can I shoot?" I whispered, "Shut up and breathe quietly. Don't you move to even kill a mosquito." There was another sampan and another. I cut the radio off for fear someone might call as these VC were passing only feet from our position. We counted sampan after sampan, far too many for us to take on. Some had one man paddling a load of what we guessed were supplies, and other boats carried three men. It was a frightening, nerve-racking time.

We waited until all the sampans were past and we were satisfied that no more were coming up the creek. I then turned the radio on and fired some of the barrages we had set up earlier. The time using a map along with the artilleryman had made the artillery rounds explode where these VC likely were. The artillery fired barrage after barrage. We did not sleep that night, not a wink. We never knew if the artillery hit the VC or not. My green radio operator learned a valuable lesson that night: do not shoot until you are sure you can win. That was one of Mosby's cardinal rules, and it was one of the VCs' as well.

The CO, having heard our radio transmissions through the night, ordered us to go back to where we had landed and catch a landing craft out. Later, we understood that the artillery used the data we brought back to pound these VCs' island positions.

During these last few weeks in country, I overheard a conversation between two of our Lieutenants. One said words to the effect, "Why don't I put you in for a Bronze Star?" "For what?" his companion asked. "I can think of something, and you put me in for one?" "That sounds like a plan," was the response. This was no joke and no joking matter. Since that day, anytime I see an officer sporting a Bronze Star, I wonder if he really did something beyond the call or if he simply had a "good buddy."

Finally, it was Newman's and my last night in combat. We both went to our platoon leader and said that our replacements were ready to lead our squads, and we were too nervous to take our squads out. The two of us would borrow a machine gun from someone who was in for the night and go with the group the Lieutenant was taking out. He said okay. Our group went out, patrolled, and set up for the night in an old Japanese bunker. There were a number of rifle slots and machine gun positions in the bunker. We set up looking out the one with the best field of view and knew that we could move to any of the other positions quickly if necessary. I was on the gun. Newman was to my side with several cans of ammo ready. I would have pitied anyone who came after us that night. We were both on edge and did not close an eye that night. Daylight came and it was back to the village. We cleaned our gun like that gunner had never seen it cleaned, returned it, and turned in our gear to supply. A helicopter came. Newman had his duffel bag. All of my belongings had been lost soon after we arrived in Vietnam; I only had a shaving kit.

It was back to some kind of processing center where we turned in the clothes on our backs. Supply issued us khaki uniforms and a pair of shoes. A pay clerk swapped out our military script and paid us the balance of our pay with real greenback dollars. We had not worn underwear or socks since we got off the *Sultan* eleven months ago. Newman had some in his duffel bag, but he was smaller than I was. Supply did not have any so I remained bareback. I was able to get some socks at the little PX. We tried to sleep in the quarters they had for us but were too anxious. Early the next morning we loaded on a 707 and all was very quiet until the plane was well in the air and then, in unison, every man on the plane shouted! We were leaving Vietnam. We were alive and in one piece! Newman was going back to Tennessee and, after a brief visit home, I went to the 51st Infantry in West Germany.

The 51st was a part of NATO's answer to the Soviets and their Warsaw Pact.

On the airplane, we felt cold, it was the first time our bodies had been exposed to seventy-degree air in a year, but the stewardesses gave us blankets and we slept soundly. We stopped briefly in Japan for fuel and then off again. The only time I woke after that was when the pilot came on and said that we had planned to refuel in Hawaii but that we had had a strong tail wind since leaving Japan, and we had enough fuel to make it to Oakland without stopping. Again, a shout went up from all of the troops onboard.

Though some of us joined, Uncle Sam drafted most of us. We did our duty. We also gathered many powerful memories so quickly that our brains overflowed with much still unprocessed. I have written some of my memories but certainly not all; I hope I have given you a flavor of infantry combat and its days of heliborne assaults, amphibious assaults, infantry assaults and its nights lying in ambush with weapons ready to kill, fighting often in the mud and, most times, at close range. That was life in the 199th Light Infantry Brigade.

As for our unit, I found this information on the internet. I believe it to be correct: The 199th Light Infantry Brigade served with distinction, honor, and valor in the Republic of Vietnam from November 28th, 1966, to October 15th, 1970. Operation Fairfax commenced in December 1966 and by the end of the month had claimed 235 VC killed or captured as compared to 15 in November killed by the then tactics. By February, VC killed or captured increased to over 300 a month. The 199th training and tactics worked. During the American involvement in Vietnam, the 199th Light Infantry proved repeatedly that it was one of the finest and most professional infantry units to have ever served in the United States Army. Organized and trained specifically for Vietnam service, the 199th became the first major American unit to undergo the process of Vietnamization with ARVN (Army of the Republic of Viet Nam) forces in 1967. They were the first American brigade in U.S. military history to have an African-American as its commanding officer. They were the first unit in Vietnam to have a Chaplain awarded the Medal of Honor and the sole unit in Vietnam to earn the dubious distinction of having lost the only general officer killed in action during ground combat. Often overshadowed by the larger, more "glamorous" units and divisions that fought in Southeast Asia, less than 25,000 men ever served in the ranks of the 199th. Yet, with more than 20% casualties – 755 young heroes died with 4,679 wounded – few fought as hard or paid more. America's best gave up the flower of their youth and went to war; let us not forget their sacrifice.

My personal opinion, the 199th proved that the American Army could successfully engage and defeat guerrilla units. As for our company, we did a darn good job. However, many of us regretted what later arriving ill-trained replacement officers did. At first, they did not understand Search and Destroy tactics. While they learned to fight, their open disdain for the Vietnamese people turned many of our villagers into communist sympathizers destroying our earlier good work and destroying any chance of us being able to work effectively with South Vietnamese forces. Such bigotry has no place in the United States Army. Lessons learned: Books on guerilla warfare emphasize such things as confuse and mislead the enemy, surprise the enemy and never fight against heavy odds. Our experience taught us that the key to winning guerilla warfare: earn and continually hold the support of the population.

Chapter 14: PTSD, an Introduction

Combat was the subject of the first part of this book. In this chapter, I digress; I prepare you for the second part of the book; here, I write about a problem that many combat soldiers have faced, Post Traumatic Stress Disorder. I cover this now to make you aware of the symptoms as I recount the later decades of my life.

Constantly being missed by whizzing bullets and shrapnel, kill or be killed, may cause PTSD. It certainly did me. I do not know how anyone can be exposed to much combat, living from minute to minute for months on end, and not be changed. I am speaking of soldiers doing the fighting and the poor civilians living in the middle of a war. War is a horrible thing: maiming and killing people, destroying homes, cities, even killing livestock, all as if it is some kind of sporting event, winner take all. War works on the strongest of minds. War means more than death and physical damage to its survivors; war causes acute anxiety, and acute anxiety changes people.

In trying to understand what had changed about soldiers returning from Civil War combat, doctors coined the term "Soldier's Heart." The term described the apparent change in the former soldiers' blood pressure and pulse rate. Drunkenness was common. Indeed, so many soldiers turned to drunkenness that the temperance movement exploded. In WORLD WAR I, the term "Shell Shocked" was adapted; many believed that the constant pounding of heavy artillery on the soldiers in the trenches somehow negatively affected the nervous system causing acute anxiety. Prohibition did not stop self-medication. However, some doctors began to think that the psychological symptoms, jumpiness and reactions to unexpected loud noises, was not due to shelling but to the acute stress of combat.

Some WORLD WAR II soldiers had "combat fatigue," but were hushed about it. They often drank too much and frequently had a hard time fitting back into civilian life. Korea was a war no one really wanted to hear about; WORLD WAR II had worn folks out. Korean War prisoners were brainwashed; that somehow must have affected many other Korean War veterans. Unlike the previous American wars, in Vietnam there was no battlefront to fall back from, thus no relief. There were no rear sister units ready to replace your unit so that you could rest for a few days in the rear. For the Vietnam combat soldier, the helicopter made Vietnam different from any other war. We came to base camp exhausted only to jump on another helicopter the next day and go to another fight. Our only real time off was five days Rest and Recuperation in a peaceful place like Japan or Taiwan.

On coming home, many Americans spit upon Vietnam veterans, called us baby killers and crazies. Some Vietnam veterans sought remedy through alcohol or illegal drugs. Sometime between Vietnam and the Iraqi and Afghanistan wars, doctors began to call these acute anxiety symptoms PTSD (Post Traumatic Stress Disorder). The Veterans Administration found ways to treat the problems. The military also discovered ways to help returning Iraqi and Afghanistan veterans have a better chance of not developing PTSD. That is wonderful, for the rate of PTSD among returning Iraqi and Afghanistan veterans is roughly half that of Vietnam veterans. We have no idea how that rate of PTSD cases compares with Korea, WORLD WAR II, and certainly not for WORLD WAR I or the Civil War.

Each war is different. WORLD WAR II in Europe was different from WORLD WAR II in the Pacific. My platoon sergeant in Vietnam was a Korean War veteran. He told us that the Korean War was vastly different from the summer to the winter. The Vietnam War – what kind of war was it?

The Cold War had caused our Army to prepare to fight the Soviets. While stationed in Germany in the late 1960s, our leaders told us that, if war broke out, it would be something like WORLD WAR II in Europe, a mobile war with fronts. Even with the addition of atomic bombs, it would be a war where occupying the ground and holding that ground would be the issue. We were so married to that model of warfare that we were not prepared to fight the guerrilla warfare raging in Southeast Asia. There was no battlefront; the enemy was sometimes directly behind us, sometimes in front of us, sometimes to the right or left, and sometimes in a tunnel underneath us.

The Army realized its mistake: fine tanks, powerful artillery, armored personnel carriers, and European tactics were nearly useless against organized guerrilla warfare. Early in the war, one General said that trying to defeat the VC was like trying to sink a floating cork using a sledgehammer. It just kept bobbing back up. The Army in Vietnam then tried to use helicopter gunships and serious artillery. The guerrilla tactic that avoided these assets was for the enemy to engage allied forces at very close range. You cannot call in gunships or artillery if you are likely to slaughter yourself. My unit, the 199th Light Infantry Brigade, was among the first units formed to seek out the enemy and crush him, trained specifically to fight the close and personal combat necessary to engage such an enemy. The generals named this new tactic Search and Destroy.

Combat turned life upside down. For the infantryman, night was no longer a time to sleep but a time to be alert. The sleep we got was not in pajamas but in helmets and fatigues with utility belts in place. Even our boots remained tightly laced. What sleep we got was lying face down; our pillow was our helmet with it against the stock of our weapon. Our right arms were to the right of our weapons and our left arms to its left. A tap on the boots, the crack of a rifle, incoming fire – those were our alarm clocks. Our first waking action was to move our trigger finger into position while trying to understand the situation: where is the enemy, where is my skill and weapon needed? The riflemen had their job, the automatic riflemen had theirs, the grenadiers another job, the radio operator still another, and so forth. The machine gun was the most devastating weapon in the infantry platoon. Carrying it meant a gun crew had to move to the thick of the fighting while the enemy was anxious to shut that big gun down. The radio operator and our leaders were next in line on the enemy's favored kill list.

An artilleryman who was in the central highlands at about the same time I was in the Delta recounted how his battery was on one hilltop for a few days, maybe a couple of weeks, before the helicopters came and moved them to another hilltop. On each hilltop it was the same: they barely had time to dig in and fill sandbags before the enemy's first mortar rounds landed. The forward observer quickly called in a fire mission. Avoiding mortar shell explosions and shrapnel as best they could, by the time they got rounds off, the enemy had left. This would happen at any hour of the day or night, no warning. It was maddening, and then the helicopters showed up again to take them to another hilltop.

The soldiers who ferried us around, the Huey helicopter jockeys, received fire daily. They rode these ships of war with distinction. There was no armor in those early Hueys. Two former crew chiefs told me that the Army issued flak jackets to the crews with orders to wear them, but they sat on them instead. Why? The most nightmarish fear a young soldier had was getting his penis shot off.

Sitting on that flak jacket was their only protection against an upcoming bullet and that horrible fate. You can live with one less hand or one less foot, but life loses some of its zest with one less dingaling.

Even soldiers in "safe areas" were not secure. I have a friend, a helicopter mechanic, who saw only one night of combat. In his first ten months in Vietnam, he had not seen a single action, then one night the enemy overran their group. Their barracks were burned, helicopters were destroyed, and friends were killed. He lived only because the first round wounded him so badly that the enemy thought him dead.

Civilians are about building some part of the economy, but combat is about destroying. Civilian life is organized, it has times and places for activities, it flows. Combat is about trying to control chaos. The prime difference: civilian life is about living; combat is about killing. There is no music on the drive to work, only gunfire and exploding artillery. The smells are not of flowers but of some poor man's torn out guts. It's kill or be killed; that's the savagery of Vietnam I remember.

Strange as it may seem, there was another difference; I made many friends in Vietnam, some very close friends, yet I left not wanting to ever see any of them again. The only piece of memorabilia I carried home was one picture, that of me with some village children. A friend snapped that picture during one of those few minutes when there was a bit of joy.

Chapter 15: Home and on to West Germany

We slept most of the way on the flight from Vietnam to Oakland. We boarded a bus that took us to a military depot. The men who were getting out of the service and went one way. Those of us still in the service got showers, turned in our khaki short-sleeve uniforms, and Uncle Sam issued a new set of dress greens complete with all of the appropriate patches and ribbons. I still did not have underwear. The sergeant in charge of the place told us that, "Things have changed since you guys left the States. Do not be downtown in uniform and stay away from hippies." Uniforms were the only clothes we had, and to ask men in their early twenties not to be downtown looking for female companionship after being gone for a year – yaa, sure. We were going downtown or die trying.

Another young sergeant and I got a cab and went to a place downtown I had frequented when stationed at Fort Ord. We ended up meeting two nice hippie girls who we were with until the place closed at two in the morning. We had a lot of fun; kissed the girls good-bye and got a little sleep at a downtown hotel. The next morning, I went to rent a car so that I could go see one of my old buddies from North Carolina State University. Even though I had more than a thousand dollars in cash, Hertz would not rent to me because I was not an officer. Avis did. Years later when I was in business and did a great deal of traveling, I never rented from Hertz; I rented from Avis.

My old buddy was in the Marines; he, his wife and baby daughter were stationed at a Naval facility near Vallejo. It would be great to see them. We were dear friends, and I had double dated with him and his wife in college. He was on duty mid-day when I arrived at their house, so his wife and baby went with me to a nice men's store in Vallejo. There I purchased several sets of underwear, shoes, socks, a pair of nice trousers, a shirt, a sweater, and a suitcase to put my dress greens in. When my dear old friend got home from work, we visited and swapped memories well into the night. The next morning, it was into my civilian clothes and to the airport.

At the airport, I purchased a ticket and went to a GI place the USO had set up to wait for my departure. There, I saw the first American television news I had seen in more than a year. CBS had a number of stories about the war; that sergeant at the depot two evenings ago was right, things had changed. The way the reporters talked and what they covered in the news disturbed me.

My plane left on time. Upon landing in Charlotte, Mom and my sister picked me up at the airport. Sister was home from college for the weekend. One of my grandfathers had died while I was gone. I was close to him and Mom said they did not want to upset me while I was overseas, so they decided to wait until I was home to tell me. I had my own story; I showed them my Purple Heart and said I did not tell you about this for the same reason.

I had a couple of weeks before I had to report to the 51st Infantry in West Germany. My dad was doing well and back at work. Mom was busy with my growing brothers and my sister ended her weekend and went back to college. During those weeks at home, I saw a few of my old pals and dated some old girlfriends, but I had changed. I ended up running around with some soldiers from Fort Bragg; one of the Airborne units and their Special Forces contingent were on maneuvers near my home in the Uwharrie National Forest. I even helped one of the Special Forces guys find a place to hide what was supposed to be a downed pilot in enemy territory. Having spent all of my young life in that forest, I knew every inch of it. I showed the Special Forces an ideal place to bushwhack the opposition as they went to and from their headquarters. I was very much on edge and ready to fight even if it was only training. It just seemed natural to be with these troops. Frankly, it excited me, made me ready to leave home for West Germany.

I flew to New York City, ate a good dinner, and took in a show. The next afternoon, I checked in at Fort Dix. Very quickly, a sergeant gave me a platoon of privates who had finished training and were to go to West Germany. My job was to make sure they and their paperwork boarded the plane and got to Rhine-Main Germany. In West Germany, I turned the new soldiers over to a corporal and picked up train tickets to Erlangen where the 51st was stationed.

It was cold. My body had made little adjustment from the heat of Vietnam; I had on underwear, wool socks, long underwear, my winter dress uniform, a heavily lined topcoat, and a hat – everything Uncle Sam had issued me – and I was still shivering. The wind was blowing so hard that the snow was falling sideways. However, once in the heated compartment on the train, I was fine. Riding along, I could see West Germany; the snow-covered hills, pastures and forestland were more than beautiful. The small villages, their walls, the architecture of the homes, their frame and stucco construction, and the narrow streets were completely new to me. There was no war. Even as darkness fell early in this northern latitude, I could not take my eyes off the train's large window; I was in a place that I had read about in history books. In storybooks, castles were make-believe, but they really exist in Europe.

By the time I arrived in Erlangen, the snow had stopped; it was a cold, crisp night. The stars were out. They were beautiful, yet not nearly as many were visible as were in the rice paddies of Vietnam. There had been no background lights in rice paddies; in the long nights waiting in bushwhack with my eyes well adjusted to the dark, I could see the stars by what seemed like millions.

I found a phone booth and called the CQ (Charge of Quarters). He sent a three-quarter- ton truck to pick me up. Once on the post, the sergeant on duty quickly took me to the headquarters billets, gave me a room, sheets, and blankets. I asked where the NCO club was and went there; I was famished. The food was good; the conversation was easy and enjoyable. This was a mechanized infantry unit. Indeed, there were no light infantry units in West Germany. I could not see running around in a cold, aluminum armored personnel carrier, exiting and charging up snow-covered frozen hills. I found out that the four-deuce (4.2-inch) mortar unit had a vacancy in its FDC (Fire Direction Center). I would be riding around inside a heated track and figuring out where to aim mortar fire. That would also give me another MOS (Military Occupational Specialty).

The next morning, it was very cold. I went to the company's chow hall. The food selection was great, everything from oatmeal to pancakes to steak and eggs, a selection of juices, chocolate milk, and good Army coffee – all excellent. It certainly beat our primary diet in Vietnam: C-rations. From there it was off to the Battalion's headquarters office to see the Sergeant Major. I told him I had heard there was an opening in the four-deuce unit. He read my records. He was a man of few words and said, "You have the scores and the background to learn the job." He sent me to see Platoon Sergeant Aldese. He was from the Philippines and turned out to be an outstanding, dedicated soldier. The battalion was soon leaving for winter maneuvers in Grafenwoehr near the Czechoslovakian border. Since I had had plenty of FO (Forward Observer, the person who calls in artillery and mortar fire) experience in Vietnam, I would start learning about the four-deuce there. Sergeant Aldese took me to the four-deuce area of the headquarters barracks. He suggested that I take the rest of the day to pick up the pass I would need to come and go from our post freely, to start the process of getting a level of security clearance needed for my new job, familiarize myself with the post, go to the PX to buy essentials, and settle into my room.

It was the middle of our Cold War with the Soviets. That evening at the NCO club, I learned that our Army had all of its units spread to many small posts all over the American Sector of West Germany. We had no large posts like in the United States. That was so that if the Soviets used atomic weapons, much of our fighting capacity would remain intact. My new post was Ferris Barracks.

Erlangen had been a garrison town in the Kingdom of Bavaria since the early 1800s. It was active in WORLD WAR I as a troop training post. Later in that war, it also served as a prisoner of war camp. After WORLD WAR I was over, it remained a garrison, though much smaller due to the Versailles Treaty. Hitler started his buildup in 1935, and Ferris Barracks was a part of that. The Waffen SS and its support units occupied Ferris Barracks during WORLD WAR II. The men who were telling me this did not know the name of the post before WORLD WAR II ended, for we renamed the post for Second Lieutenant Ferris who died near there in WORLD WAR II. There were still holes in some of the buildings where Allied fighter planes had strafed the barracks near the end of WORLD WAR II. We still had some WORLD WAR II soldiers in the army, and they would not allow anyone to repair those bullet holes; their memories were still strong. One of those men was a Master Sergeant I met. As a hobby, he took care of a Sherman Tank left over from that war. It was in perfect condition. He let me ride with him in a parade once. It was something I will long remember.

The SS was special in Hitler's eyes; that was why the barracks were the best billets I saw during my time in the service. The building I was in was three stories high with four stories underground. The boilers for the entire post were in the deepest basement in our building. Educated as an engineer, that interested me. From these boilers, underground pipes distributed steam and hot water to every building in the complex. We had the same arrangement where I had gone to college except our boilers were above ground. One of the older NCOs told me that there were tunnels under the entire complex connecting all of the buildings and connecting our post with some others in the area. These connecting tunnels were able to handle Panzer movements.

I was unable to confirm that there were tunnels connecting our post to other posts in the area; however, sometime later when I was on CQ at the same time as my platoon leader, we went down to the deepest basement and found a tunnel leading toward the next barracks. With big flashlights in hand, we entered the tunnel. However, we did not go but twenty feet or so down that tunnel until we

ran into a tall, chain-link gate an engineering unit
had put in place near the end of the war. Two
padlocks secured the gate. There were large black-
on-red warning signs on the gate and both walls
telling us to go no further, for the place was booby-
trapped. Hitler had planned to fight to the last man,
and his SS was prepared to back him. We shone our
lights down the tunnel past the gate and could see
that the tunnel opened up. There we could see a
German half-trick; this was twenty-three years after
WORLD WAR II ended, and the place was still
dangerous. I would have expected water to be in
this old tunnel; the fact that there was none was a
tribute to the German engineers who designed and
built them. Such a waste.

On my first day on duty, I met our Platoon
Leader and the other members of the platoon. I was
surprised that our platoon was only about one-third
strength due to the drain the Vietnam War placed on
military resources. In our upcoming maneuvers, we
would have to qualify our platoon. To fill our
platoon for our qualification shoot, we would have
some of the most experienced GIs from the 81-
millimeter mortar platoons join us taking the platoon
up to strength. I also learned that almost all of our
armored personnel carriers, while they would run,
had some mechanical problems. There was no
money for repair parts. The Pentagon was spending
most of its money in Vietnam; we would have to
make do.

At the NCO club, I found that the nearest
place I would enjoy was a place full of history,

Nuremberg. It was only a short ride by train. My first Saturday morning off I went. Upon exiting the train station on a low hill, I could see the walls that surrounded the old city as well as Nuremberg Castle on the highest hill in the city. The two castles I had gotten glimpses of on my train ride to Erlangen were small. Nuremberg's castle was expansive; its wall enclosed several square miles. I walked to the castle, and by Sunday evening I had walked around much of the old city. I had a thousand questions.

Nuremberg was a city-state dating from around 1,000 CE. It had never been defeated in a war and, because of that, it was to be the future home of Hitler's capitol, one of his occult beliefs. Over the next fifteen months, I saw the Stadium where Hitler held his rallies, I saw Hitler's incomplete capitol with airstrip; it was then a fertilizer factory. I saw the Palace of Justice, site of the post-WORLD WAR II Nazi war crimes trials. The German National Museum was full of history and a Gutenberg Bible. There was a toy museum (Nuremberg had once been a major manufacturing town for toys). I went to the best toy store I have ever visited, and on and on. Not only that, but I took two 30-day leaves and went to England, saw London, some of its museums, and Stratford on Avon, Shakespeare's home. It was great to be able to talk to the English girls; I dated a few. I also went to Belgium, Switzerland, Austria, and Italy as well as other West German towns like Rothenberg. My experience here in Europe taught me that I was a foreigner in other peoples' countries. I learned that people enjoyed talking about their culture and history. I became a good listener. All of this was to pay big dividends later in life, for I was to travel to twenty-six countries in my business career.

However, I felt safe only when I had a weapon. A friend and I were in London and taking the last train of the night back to our hotel when we prevented some trouble. We got on the Underground (the English subway) and sat at the end of the car facing so that we could see the entire length of the car. There were only three other people on the train. The most distant was a male cross-dresser; next sat a young man sporting a school scarf, and nearest to us was a young woman. All was fine until two or three stops later when, at the other end of the car, two half-drunk hoodlums boarded. As soon as the car started moving, they got up from their seats and grabbed at the cross dresser. He pulled free and quickly moved further down the car. Then they slapped the books out of the lap of the student and headed for the lady. My friend and I reacted spontaneously. We both stood up and flipped out our switchblades. We then said in a loud voice, "Boys, we are Americans, and we will not put up with your violence. You will exit at the next stop." They immediately sat down. We folded our knives, put them back in our pockets, and sat down. At the next stop, the two boys bolted out of the car. I did not know my friend carried a switchblade and he did not know I carried one. We were just soldiers trained to react in violent situations.

I used violence to settle a problem only twice in my civilian life; in that switchblade incident and in the fifth grade when a bully attacked me; then it was fight or be pounded. Maybe my hatred of violence is why I have PTSD. My duty to country wrestles against my basic non-confrontational personality, my desire for peace.

Unlike Vietnam where I had no personal possessions, in Germany I had my own room complete with a wall locker and a footlocker. We could own things. I purchased some very nice tailor-made clothes, a radio that received not only AM and FM, but also two shortwave bands and longwave. That enabled me to hear not only Armed Forces Radio, but also BBC and several English-language stations. I also acquired a fine camera that I carried as I traveled about. When I left Germany, I had a shoebox full of the sights and scenes of Europe from Stafford on Avon to Venice. "Join the Army and see the world." I did.

Today, worldwide communications are only a quick phone call away; it was not that way when I was young. In my hometown, even calling to the next town seven miles away required a pricy long-distance call. You had to dial zero and get an operator to connect you. Calling internationally was very expensive and required that I go to the telephone office in downtown Erlangen, go into one of their several phone booths, call an operator, and wait minutes for the connections to be made. That meant that, in an emergency, I could call home. In Vietnam, the only outside communications were via the U.S. mail. You have to have lived a while to really appreciate progress.

On duty, I found that most of the soldiers in West Germany were in for their two-year draft obligation and were not serious. They seemed oblivious to the idea of war. While I enjoyed being in Europe and traveling, inside I was rarely comfortable, always on guard, and always ready for war. I was accustomed to my combat views and fears; I just did not fit in with peacetime soldiers. I was still mentally in the war, hyper-alert, nervous. On whom could I depend if war with the Soviets broke-out? Consequently, I made friends with only a small number of older NCOs who had some kind of war experience. I understood them and they understood me. I became close to several.

My best friend, Platoon Sergeant Hillbun, was a well-experienced NCO. He had been one of a number of GIs shipboard and ready to join in the Bay of Pigs Cuba invasion when President Kennedy canceled the invasion. Sergeant Hillbun and I loved German food and in Erlangen there were several great restaurants. My favorite food was the simplest, Nuremberger bratwurst with brown bread, mustard, and sauerkraut. Then there were the fast-food places – these were nothing like in America. They sold shish kebabs, all kinds of wurst (sausages), and breads. Always fresh baked, the breads were good by themselves. A typical sandwich consisted of buttered bread with a slice of some kind of spiced meat loaf in the middle. Their pastries were delicious and baked daily. They were very different from American pastries; they were not nearly so sweet. The results: you could taste the other delicious ingredients such as fresh cream. The Germans also had some of the best roasted chicken; it would melt in your mouth. My favorite restaurant was in Nuremberg. It was in a cellar just off Konigstrasse not far from the train station. I first went there because Hitler had spoken there in the 1930s, and I found the food to be terrific. Such a wonderful place was to be my home for fourteen or fifteen months.

Chapter 16: Field and Garrison Duty

After a little practice with our few four-deuce
soldiers and the GIs from the 81-mm mortars, it was
off to Grafenwoehr for our qualification shoot.
Grafenwoehr was an artillery firing range used by
the German Army before and during WORLD WAR
II. It was darn cold. We wore all of our winter gear
to include fur-lined hats with earflaps down,
facemasks, wool field trousers, wool blouses, a
parka, wool socks, and cold weather boots all over
our regular fatigues and long underwear. On our
hands, we wore a pair of wool gloves, covered by a
pair of leather gloves, covered by a lined mitten with
a lined finger hole to enable one to use his trigger
finger with gloves and mittens on. That was the
only convenience, for all of that clothing limited our
flexibility greatly. Our jeeps were set up for
wartime, no windshield or canvas top; both the
driver and the passengers had to wear goggles when
driving. Sandbags covered the entire bottoms of the
jeeps just in case we were to run over a landmine.
There were no simulated landmines in our training
area; the sandbags were there in case the Soviets
attacked. I thought to myself, an under-strength
army with equipment that needs repair, but we had
sandbags in our jeeps. I guess the sandbags gave the
appearance of a unit that was ready to fight. I did
not feel comfortable; what if the Soviets did attack?
The Soviets had some darn fine tanks, a number

with 122-mm cannons. Our best tank, the M-60A1, only had a 105-mm cannon.

Our first morning in Grafenwoehr, the staff sergeant in charge of our FDC and I left to go to the lookout post from which I would be calling in our shots. I was driving; the staff sergeant asked me to stop at the Class 6 Store, the liquor store. He said that he did not drink on duty but we would need a little reinforcement on top of that mountain. I was uncomfortable with that, but he was the one in charge. He purchased a bottle of brandy. Up we went to the military crest of this high mountain and to a reinforced bunker. The military crest is as high as you can go on a mountain and not have the enemy see you silhouetted against the sky.

The wind was howling. From this bunker, we had an excellent view of the firing range. I had to urinate and went behind the bunker to relieve myself. My urine froze nearly instantly; that's cold. I poked my finger out of the finger hole in my mittens to adjust my binoculars. We were able to get the map out of the wind by moving to a corner of the bunker and there orient the map. The Mekong Delta was flat; here there were many changes in altitude; even moving our fire a few meters could make a large change in the beaten zone. The staff sergeant gave some rules to follow to compensate for terrain altitude changes. I asked many questions and studied the map in detail. He had been here a number of times and told me where to expect I would likely be calling shots. He also told me that he had just learned that we would be firing at the same time 8-inch howitzers were. Several high-ranking officers, including some generals, would be observing.

The next day, I was on top of that mountain where I met a first lieutenant and his driver. The lieutenant was the FO for the 8-inch howitzers. We got our fire missions over our radios. They were identical. In Vietnam we used yards and miles; in Germany we used meters and kilometers. Using a conversion chart, I was able to do my job. Within a minute, we were both on our radios calling in fire. Now, 8-inch howitzers fire rounds that weigh around 200 pounds each. A 200-pounds round of high explosive makes a hole big enough to swallow a tank. Four-deuce mortars fire rounds that weigh around twenty-five pounds. However, 8-inch howitzers fire three rounds every two minutes. Four-deuce mortars, once the tube (the barrel) is hot, fires eighteen rounds a minute. Further, since mortar rounds come out of the tube at one-third the speed of howitzers rounds, the rounds' skin does not need to be thick to withstand the less powerful blast shock that sends it out of its barrel. That translates into more exploding power per pound of round. There were two howitzers and our four mortars firing that day. I was pleasantly shocked to see how much damage we did because of our rate of fire. We were putting 144 rounds on the target area to the howitzers' three rounds. We had excellent scores that day. It was the first thing I had seen in West Germany that gave me faith that the Four-Deuce could indeed take on the Soviets' infantry, and the 8-inch could take on its tanks.

For the rest of our time at Grafenwoehr, we were playing war games and living outside much of the time. My first night out was a learning experience. Our FDC track had a crew of three. Our heated track was perfect for sleeping those three. However, soon after dark, in came our platoon leader and his driver. Surprise! They were also going to sleep in the track. That meant we would all have to sleep sitting up. An old Boy Scout, I grabbed my sleeping gear and decided that I had rather sleep in the snow. I found a level spot near our track and kicked a clear place in the snow, blew up my air mattress, rolled my sleeping bag out, and covered it with my poncho. I then took off my boots and outer field gear, put those items in my sleeping bag to act as a pillow and crawled in. I slept like a baby. The next morning, I awoke covered by three or four inches of snow with but a little hole looking skyward that my exhaled breath had kept open. My body heat had warmed my outer gear. Somehow, I got my outer gear on in the tight confines of the mummy bag and came out well refreshed. After rolling up my gear, I went back to the track to find four miserable men. They had slept little.

After a few days, it warmed up enough in the afternoons that some of the frozen ground turned to slick mud for a few hours. Our battalion had a lieutenant colonel fresh from the Pentagon. He was up for colonel, but first he had to have a field command; this unit was it. He insisted that, with the warmer weather, we take off our arctic boots and field trousers and parkas and just wear our regular field jackets and leather boots. A number of soldiers got wet feet and all were too cold – too cold to pay attention to what we were doing. Meanwhile, he rode around in a heated jeep. Even with my limited time in the service, I agreed with my friend, Platoon Sergeant Hillbun; every officer needs to spend at least a year as an enlisted man before being commissioned.

Meanwhile, Sergeant Aldese taught me that staying warm in this severely cold weather required a heavy breakfast. While at Grafenwoehr, our mess sergeant made sure we had pancakes, several kinds of meat, eggs, cereal, milk, juice, and plenty of hot coffee; I ate some of all of it. On those mornings that we slept in the field, I ate two boxes of C-rations, 2,400 calories, for breakfast. After a few weeks at Grafenwoehr, I was beginning to adapt to the weather, and then it was back to Erlangen to clean all of our gear and say good-bye to the men from the 81-mm mortar platoons; they were great.

My first weekend back in Erlangen, I was off to Nuremberg. Sergeant Hillbun asked if I would take his newest soldier downtown and keep him out of trouble until he learned his way around. That was a good thing. Not speaking the language of one's host country and not knowing the bad parts of a town, one can get into trouble and never know it until it is too late. I was happy to introduce the man to Germany.

The man had just returned from Vietnam. We spent most of the day in Nuremberg castle and ate supper near there. By that time, it was dark. As we walked down Konigstrasse, we ran up on four German students who had had quite a bit to drink and were walking arm in arm down the street singing American songs. We joined in as they sang "We Shall Overcome", and they asked us to join them. We locked arms and went along singing with them. We stopped so they and my companions could refuel. They all spoke English well but did not understand the meaning of the slang words and phrases in several songs. We explained the songs' lingo.

One of these young men, Hans Schmitt, was deeply interested in America, and I was deeply interested in his country. I met him the next day for lunch, and over the next twelve months, we became friends. He and his mother took me to their house for dinner several times. She said, through Hans, that I was the first American she had met since the end of the war. At that time, three GIs had her fix some food for them and then made her eat it first to see if it was poisoned. I could not imagine putting such a fine lady through such a test.

Hans and his friends also introduced me to a number of German girls; they would not have had anything to do with a GI any other way. My new friends taught me enough German to get around. We also went camping in Austria, went to parties together, and he showed me things in Nuremberg that I would have never experienced had it not been for him. Later, after I was back in the States and married, Hans came to America. We took him camping; helped him buy a car, and he drove around America meeting one of my first cousins in California. Having studied in Germany, she was happy to show him the west coast. Later, Hans came to America several more times. Once, after he was married. He and his wife spent a part of their honeymoon with us. My wife and family went to Europe for three weeks and stayed with Hans and his wife for a few days.

Many Germans were quite nice to me, particularly the Germans my age. However, there were Germans who did not like Americans in their country. I understood that. There were also a few die-hard Nazis. One day while walking by myself, a man on the other side of the street started goose stepping and singing at the top of his voice a Nazi song, *Die Fahe hoch die Reihen fest geschlossen* (The flag is high, our ranks are closed). He obviously wanted my attention, for he marched and sang until I was out of his sight. I understood how The Treaty of Versailles burdened Germany with a tremendous war debt and then came the Great Depression. People were starving. Desperation let a criminal, Hitler, give them hope as he bit by bit seized total control. Under similar conditions, it could happen in America. To think otherwise is ignorant.

In truth, the values of the people that I met in Germany, both young and old, were actually similar to our American values. I loved the German people and the German culture. People have asked me *why* the German people tolerated the death camps. I asked myself that and studied that question for years. In that process, I also asked myself *why* my great grandparents tolerated slavery. I asked myself, since slavery ended, *why* the generations, including my own, tolerated segregation. South Africa tolerated apartheid. *Why?* This is my opinion: We understand our world through the interpretation of our culture at a particular time and place in history, our era. That era gives us particular prejudices and biases. We cannot understand things that are outside of those prejudices and biases, outside of our worldview. That is to say, history does not belong to us; rather, we belong to it.

Ordinary people belonging to their history committed the monstrous evil acts in the examples I have cited: death camps, slavery, segregation, and apartheid. These people lived in political systems that took advantage of our human tendency to feel superior to those with whom we differ. They did not have to have empathic feelings or consideration for those they considered to be inferior classes. The "superior" failed to treat the "inferior" the way they would like to be treated.

We, too, belong to the history of our time. We now see the sins of past generations clearly. I hear people judge the past by the standards of today and react with disgust, self-righteous indignation, and anger. I suggest that we must constantly be on guard for the failures of our political leaders. I suggest that future generations will likely ask *why* we tolerated this or that. We must face the truth, those who do not understand history will make similar mistakes to those of the past, only with more and more powerful technology, the results may be far worse. We human beings are the most conceited creatures on earth. We are simply not nearly as smart as we think we are. We are not gods; we are fallible creatures. We must not assume that our current society is the pinnacle of greatness; we should constantly criticize our prejudices and biases.

After I got my security clearance, I learned our army could respond to a Soviet attack with more powerful weapons than four-deuce mortars and 8-inch howitzers. The army constantly rotated nuclear weapons around many sites in West Germany. This was to prevent the Warsaw Pact from knowing the numbers and locations of these weapons. I was one of several NCOs and a number of enlisted men who took turns guarding nuclear weapons storage sites. This was serious business. All sites had a contingent of soldiers on duty twenty-four hours a day. When it was our time to guard a site, an officer inspected us and reviewed with us our special orders, special orders that included shooting anyone who came near the storage area. Closed trucks always rode us to a site for our three days of duty. A series of NATO high chain-link fence lines topped with concertina razor wire surrounded all sites. Housed in concrete bunkers inside the fence lines, it would have taken many armed men to unseat us.

    While in Grafenwoehr, I met a very interesting Platoon Sergeant. Some of the things he told me were as frightening as were the Nazi death camps. He had a CBR MOS (Chemical, Bacteriological, and Radiological warfare Military Occupational Specialty). Chemical, Bacteriological, and Radiological warfare are the weapons of the next world war. He told me that a two-week school on the subject was about to start and that I should put in for it. I did. I had grown up when people were building fall-out shelters. As a child, our teachers taught us to crawl under our desks should the Soviets attack us, or, if at home, go to our basement. At that same time, we had a Strategic Air Command that had planes loaded with atomic bombs in the air twenty-four hours a day. Therefore, I went to that CBR School frightened of nuclear warfare. I left the school thinking bacteriological warfare was far worse, far more powerful, and far more likely.

    In a bacteriological war, the enemy would have vaccinated its population against the bacterial weapon they were going to release. Then, five or six men would release an airborne bacteriological agent into the heating and air-conditioning intakes at several international airports. The bacteriological agent they released would go unnoticed through the air into travelers' lungs. It would take several days for any symptoms to arise; meanwhile the travelers would be infecting virtually everyone they met even before symptoms would show. The agent would be self-replicating and lethal. In but a few weeks, a pandemic would have started. The agent would kill a very high percentage of the population. After the pandemic, the victor would send troops to the nation they wanted to take over and bury the dead. Then the victor would have that nation's houses unharmed, cars in their driveways, and all of the nation's wealth intact. It was possible in 1968; what capabilities are currently available to evil people and self-righteous nations today.

I got back to Erlangen and found myself appointed NCOIC (Non Commissioned Officer In Charge) of the battalion rifle team. The rifle team consisted of the best shots in the battalion. The lieutenant colonel was determined to win the upcoming competition against teams from units all over the American sector. We had one advantage; our shooting range would be the sight of the competition. Our battalion's armorer did a great job souping up our M-14s. They were the pick of the arms rooms and barely legal in all regards plus had only 2 ½-pound trigger pulls. We had all the ammo we could shoot. For a month, our team was on the range by 0800 and shot until 1700. We stayed on the range over lunch, for the mess sergeant brought us a hot lunch every day. When the days of the competition came, a large number of teams arrived. The audience consisted of a number of high-ranking officers plus a few well-wishers. After three days of shooting, we came in second overall. The lieutenant colonel wanted us to be first and showed his disappointment by not congratulating us; indeed, he did not even speak to us. The sergeant major and several other of our senior NCOs did come and shake all of our team members' hands saying, "Great job."

Meanwhile, in January of 1968, we had the Prague Spring. Alexander Dubcek became First Secretary of Czechoslovakia and started reforms that gave citizens more rights. The Soviets did not like this. In the late summer of 1968, the Soviets along with other members of the Warsaw Pact invaded Czechoslovakia and seized control of its government putting their hand picked people in charge. We loaded our tracks with our basic load of ammunition and went near the Czech border to help any escaping Czechs. We were ready just in case the Soviets' aspiration included West Germany. At the NCO club, I learned the brass said that it would only take seven days for the Soviets and their flunkies to push us to the English Channel. It was a frightening time. I started having nightmares. I figured that after our first resistance, things would break down quickly. I made up my mind that life in a Soviet prisoner of war camp was not for me. I remembered reading about a few GIs, in WORLD WAR II's Pacific Theater, who evaded capture during the early part of the war and were able to continue fighting with partisans. I made up my mind that I would attempt the same. I knew I would not be alone. I would wait a few days, come out, help form and train West German freedom fighters. It sounds silly today, but that is exactly what I thought and planned; after all, the army had trained me to think that way, and I was experienced in guerrilla warfare.

I had earned a reputation for being a straight-laced, well-disciplined soldier; sometimes, that was a burden. One day, Sergeant Aldese brought me two men. They were to be court-martialed the next morning. "Take care of them," he said. I spoke nicely to them and took them to the supply room to get bedding and then to one of our unoccupied squad rooms on the third floor. As soon as we were alone in the room, one of them said to me, "If you mess with us we will throw you out of that window. When they asked us what happened, we will say, 'He just went crazy and jumped out of the window.'" I responded, "Look, right now I am the closest thing to a friend you have. Do not mess that up." They were not pleasant but at least did not threaten me again. The next morning, I walked them over to battalion headquarters for the court-martial proceedings. I left them there and went on to my work.

Late in the afternoon, Sergeant Aldese called me and said, go to the arms room and draw a pistol and a few magazines. Load the magazines and go see the sergeant major. He has a prisoner for you to take care of; the court-martial found one of the men guilty of beating and raping a German girl. The sergeant major wants you to watch him until the MPs (Military Police) get here.

When I arrived at the sergeant major's office, he said that I was to take the man to the CQ room and watch him until the MPs arrived. Further, he said that since I was not an MP, I was under different rules than the MPs were. He said words to the effect, "You are to consider this man very dangerous and likely to run. If he does, shoot him. Do you understand?" "Yes, sergeant major." I gave the man an evil smile, pulled my forty-five out of its holster and slammed a magazine into the pistol. I then chambered a round and holstered my weapon. With the evil smile still on my face, I said to the man, "Please cooperate and make this easy on both of us. If you do run, I will send you to hell. Do you understand?" The man was silent, got up and did what I said until we got outside. There he began telling me that his buddies would get even with me, but he kept walking. Thankfully, the MPs showed up soon after we arrived at the CQ room.

Our lieutenant colonel was relieved of his command just before I finished my time in West Germany. He got drunk and hit a sign that fell and severely injured a German woman. I do not think anyone was sorry to see him go. Meanwhile, Hans and my other friends gave me a going away party. The next morning, I was off to Rhine-Main to board a plane for the United States of America and back to North Carolina State University.

Chapter 17: Back in Civilian Life

The army honorably discharged me at Fort
Dix just a few days before spring semester started. I
flew home, spent a little time saying hello to the
folks, and did exactly what I had planned when
joining the army. I returned to college one day
before spring semester started. I had registered for
classes and paid tuition and fees while stationed in
Germany. Being back on campus, going to classes,
staying in my old dormitory, and eating cafeteria
food three times a day was at first nostalgic, but I
soon realized how drastically the University had
changed; I had changed too. Though clean,
dormitories were never nearly spotless like army
barracks were, and the food was far short of first-
class mess hall food. Cultural shock set in.

When I left NC State University, segregation
was just ending. The campus YMCA housed a few
Afro-American students as a token of the
University's commitment to integrate the races.
Further, since its opening in 1887, NCSU had been
an all male institution and coeducation had just
begun. The very few coeds we had were married to
other NCSU students and lived on the edge of
campus with their husbands in campus duplexes. In
three years, the student body had grown from
roughly 9,000 to 11,000 and most of those 2,000
additional students were Afro-American and/or
female. The University had integrated its
dormitories and had several all female dormitories.
I had never heard of "inclusive language," yet my

English teacher insisted that I use it. It was no longer he, him, his, but he or she, him or her, his or hers. She explained the logic. After some thought, I agreed.

Removed from American society during these major societal shifts gave me a vantage point few have had. To help expose these changes, I have used the language of the times, for that language exposes drastic shifts in the worldviews. Therefore, now I shift from the language of the 1950s and 60s to the language of the 1970s.

I was more than ready to put the war behind me, adapt to a new world, and become a dedicated bookworm. Yet, I was slapped in the face with another change. The attitude towards the Vietnam War had become decidedly negative. You could not walk around the campus without having your nose rubbed in the anti-war fervor. If I remember correctly, I told only my roommate, the head of my department, and my advisor that I was a veteran. The head of my department was Dutch and a victim of Nazi occupation. My advisors shared with me that he was an infantry veteran of WORLD WAR II who fought in Germany. They both understood what war does to people. They understood my strong emotions, my desire to avoid anything associated with Vietnam. The completely uninformed anti-war crowd angered me. They spoke horribly about our boys in uniform. They called us "baby killers." While I respected and defended their right to protest peacefully, I went to great lengths to stay completely away from their gatherings. I could never watch nightly news on television: Vietnam, Vietnam, Vietnam. Once, while engrossed in a WORLD WAR II movie, I flared up and shouted at a soldier walking along a ridgeline something like, "No! Do not do that!" I guess people in the theater thought that I was a nutcase; that was embarrassing.

That first summer after going back to college, I stayed home with my parents and younger brothers, worked hard, and saved every cent I could. I also started dating my soon-to-be wife. I had known her family and her most of my life. While I was overseas, she had changed from an attractive teenager to a beautiful woman. She had lost high school classmates to "that war" and understood my pain. One day while standing with her outside her house, an old truck went by and its engine backfired. Without a thought, I had thrown her to the ground and jumped on her to protect her – I was temporarily back in combat. She understood my profound embarrassment and apology.

Dormitory life and I no longer fit; that fall semester, I found two ex-GIs and moved into an apartment with them. It was cheaper than living on campus. We never discussed the war, lived quietly and peacefully. We were comfortable with each other. The three of us studied hard and held down jobs. We also still got up at 0530 even without the blast of *Reveille*. I had begun receiving the GI bill. That and summer work helped me pay my way through college, but it was not nearly enough. I held down three part-time jobs, two of which were for research in my career field. I saw my wife-to-be as often as possible, but she worked near our hometown and my studies, work, and inability to afford a car kept me on campus in Raleigh most of the time.

One of those part-time jobs was to pay tremendous dividends – I wrote thirty-plus training manuals. They were much like army training manuals. I would study a machine, the operator's job, and break its operations into components. I would then decide what the person using this manual needed to know first, second, and so-forth. This involved interviewing and working with people who did the job, used the equipment. Often, it also involved studying what others had written on the subject. With the earliest manuals, I also went to several companies and actually trained people. The training manuals were simply summaries of what I had learned presented in an organized fashion. This experience was an incredible education in itself.

My grades were such that the head of the department and my advisor helped me get several scholarships. I suspect that help was in part empathic. They, too, had gone to college after their wartime experiences. They saw Ho Chi Minh and Mao Zedong as being the same kind of dictators as Benito Mussolini and Adolf Hitler. They saw the anti-war protestors as just another fad consuming a number of college kids. So did I. Then, on May 4, 1970, the Ohio National Guard killed four and wounded nine students in thirteen seconds of gunfire. The Kent State shootings were horrible.

I tried to be rational while refusing to accept that as a proper human response. I had seen too much death. Painful emotions filled my soul. These soldiers were the same ages as the students they shot. I supported the students' right to protest. I also understood how frightened the students made the young, inexperienced soldiers feel. They were not trained police; they were soldiers. Yet, the spilled blood of the young and the innocent was unacceptable. Many protestors had not understood why they were protesting. For them, it was a social experience. One of my brothers had gone to a protest or two; his explanation: "That's where the girls are." Now, serious, spontaneous protests broke out all over our nation and even on our conservative campus. Students donned black armbands as a sign of mourning. It was time for our final exams. Teachers, instructors, and professors made final exams optional. A student could take the grade he or she had as his or her final grade.

We had a number of sailors and naval officers studying on campus, they understood the gravity of the shootings and felt differently. They donned red, white, and blue armbands. In one of my classes, a social studies class, the instructor felt it appropriate for the class to discuss the Kent State shootings. After listening to students who wanted vengeance, I spoke up exposing myself as a Vietnam veteran. I asked them to understand that the National Guardsmen were not police. Soldiers used offensive weapons; their training was to kill, destroy. Police use defensive weapons; their training was about the prevention of crime and the maintenance of public order. Whoever made the decision to send Guardsmen rather than police was responsible for the killings and the pain the Guardsmen would feel until they died. Immediately, one student branded me a villain. However, I was popular among the majority of the class and they made an excuse for me. They felt that I had to feel the way I felt to cover my conscience. I regretted having opened my mouth. I took my final exams, and kept shut my mouth.

My WORLD WAR II veteran advisor had noticed I sometimes misunderstood him. I had confessed that I was having some hearing problems. He said that I should go to the Veteran's administration and they would likely give me some hearing aids. I went to the VA hospital in Durham. The man that examined my hearing was unapologetically anti-war. He smiled as he gave me the results. He said that I had definitely had some hearing loss like that caused by exposure to gunfire but it was not compensable. I said that I did not come for compensation; I had to set in the front of my classes in order to hear. He laughed at me. I did not mention Vietnam again for years.

Then there was President Nixon. He had promised "peace with honor." I still thought like an American soldier. If we were fighting against evil, and I saw for myself that we were, the only peace with honor was total victory, for only then could the Vietnamese truly have peace with liberty. As things in Vietnam dragged on, I began to realize that not all of the generals nor the President was thinking of victory. If they wanted out, then they should get out! If you want to win, invade the North. There our generals can fight the kind of war they know how to win. Oh, "We do not want another Korean War with Chinese troops blowing their bugles as waves of them charge our boys." If victory is not your goal, then pack up and leave Vietnam in the morning; do not give me that "peace with honor" nonsense. Our best and brightest are dying for your idea of honor. Get out or fight!

Finally, after three and a half years in college, three years in the army, and two and a half more years in college, I did very well, graduated with an excellent education, and had a number of exceptional job offers. By then I was married and we were expecting our first child, a girl. I chose the job that paid the highest salary.

It was great to have a good job. We moved to a small town in the Blue Ridge Mountains and went to work as an engineer for a manufacturing company. I had to go through a six-month training program that took me through every department in the company's primary factory. From there I became one of the company's engineers. Vietnam was on the news every night; it upset me, frustrated me. I lost myself in my job and my young family.

President Nixon signed into law the Occupation Safety and Health Administration and the Environmental Protection Administration in late 1970, and the first regulations came out near the end of my first year with the company, 1972. The

President of the company called me into his office and said words to the effect, "Lee, I am putting you in charge of improving company safety and meeting the new environmental standards at all of the company's plants. None of us old folks know anything about this, so you are going to have to figure this out and tell us what to do." He then handed me one book that contained the early OSHA standards and another about what the EPA expected. I read and studied the books and went to a number of seminars to learn the ins and outs of the laws and regulations. I also took pains to make friends with the people within the State and Federal governments with whom I would have to work. That turned out to be one of my best decisions because air pollution regulators worked with me to figure out how best to meet the new standards.

There was much to do at every one of our facilities. I suddenly found myself at work fifty-five to sixty hours a week and often spent time away from my family at seminars. We soon had a second child, a boy. Thank the LORD that I had married a strong young woman. She was a full-time busy Mom. I often got home after the children were in bed and left before anyone got up in the morning.

My old DI from AIT had emphasized, "Learn the job, do the job, teach the job and move on." That is exactly what I had done as a machine gunner and a squad leader. I did the same thing with OSHA and EPA. I ended up having someone at each location in the company who was taking care of safety and the environmental regulations and

reports. I simply became the person they would call
when they were in a tight spot.

That paid off. One day, the president of the
company invited me into his shiny new Cadillac,
and took me to a large overgrown field. My wife
and I had one compact station wagon with which we
were very careful. My boss drove that big Cadillac
down an old sawmill road with overgrowth and tree
limbs scraping the sides and top of his car without
thinking about the damage he was doing to it. The
branches scraping the car sounded like a kid
scraping a chalkboard with his fingernails; it made
my skin crawl. There, in that field, the man gave me
his next project; he wanted me to build and start a
factory there. I worked with consultants, engineers,
local officials, State and Federal regulators, and
contractors as we planned and built the plant. The
project took me to many machine-manufacturing
plants in our country and back to Germany buying
the equipment people would need to make products
in the new plant. Finally, I was the plant manager
responsible for training the employees and starting
the operation. It took much time and required long
hours seven days a week. I was at work by 6:30
a.m. and home late. Even on Sunday, I would get
up, dress for church, and go to work. I would go
back home in time to take my wife and children to
Sunday school and church, eat lunch with them, and
then go back to work.

Saigon fell and we were out of Vietnam. I
was both glad that our boys would now quit dying
and emotionally shaken that America and South

Vietnam were defeated. I was hurt, disgusted, angry, mad – words still fail me. That's part of the reason I am writing this book: it still hurts. Our nation's sacrifice came to more than 58,000 dead, more 153,000 wounded, and almost 1,600 missing in action. While estimates vary widely, the total deaths of South Vietnamese, South Koreans, Australians, Filipinos, New Zealanders, Siamese, Taiwanese, and Canadians, including soldiers and civilians, exceeded 1,500,000. What was the "honor" in all of that? Both our political leaders and our generals failed! I just wanted to be alone.

The plant was slowly coming along. Some of our employees were becoming leaders and assuming responsibility. We were accomplishing what the President asked my employees and me to do, but the long hours cost me my health; I ended up in the hospital with pneumonia. Indeed, the doctor said that I was one tough SOB, for I had been walking around with it for weeks. I was out of work for nearly a month. Once well, my doctor, a wise man, said that I could slow down, work something like a regular workweek and start taking some time off or die. The company only granted two weeks of vacation a year, and I had not taken any vacation since the plant project started.

Soon after being back at work, another plant manager came to me and said that we, referring to the company leadership, counted my time off with pneumonia as my vacation for the next few years. Not only had they delegated a conversation they should have had with me, they were obviously unaware of how hard I had worked for them, that I had had no vacation for a couple of years. This great job was just like Vietnam, a lot of sacrifice for a kick in testes. The doctor was plain, make time for my health or die.

What I had been doing at this company had brought me notoriety in industry. People had called me wanting me to go to work for them. I had repeatedly turned those calls politely down. I could no longer; I had a young family that needed a husband and a father. I phoned one of those who had called, and the next weekend I flew to Chicago to see the man. He owned several operations, one in East Tennessee. The money was much better and, from his description of the job and the outcome he wanted, I could do it and lead a more normal life. It was a good decision. Unfortunately, the damage to my right lung was so great that less than five years later, I had the bottom lobe of my right lung removed. The remainder of that lung had a condition known as bronchiectasis; however, my natural tenacity enabled me to learn to control that and some years of success followed.

Chapter 18: Nightmares

My advisor in college had many years of experience in industry. Further, the Engineering College of the University encouraged professors to do consulting in order to keep up with the problems and solutions in industry. This practice enriched instruction and encouraged research to find better solutions to those problems. My advisor, who did consulting, said that he found that 95% of the problems he was asked to solve were basic; they were not mind-boggling. People become so busy with problems they forget the fundamentals. He preached, when faced with a problem look first at the basics we are teaching, there you will find solutions.

When I arrived at my new job in East Tennessee that is exactly what I found. They had modern, well-maintained machinery in a modern, well-laid-out plant. They had plenty of business. They had knowledgeable people. They were missing the most basic management tool in industry; they had no scheduling system. The results were chaos on the factory floor, horrible morale, high employee turnover, and angry customers.

I went over every order in-house. I put them in order by the date the customer had asked for delivery. We had several weeks' worth of incomplete orders and two weeks' worth of work due the following week. Every order had the invoice amount posted on it. The quickest scheduling system I could come up with was simply the daily dollars in shipments we needed to earn a small profit. I called the vice president of sales and my own sales manager to a meeting and showed them the problem. I knew that most customers had two things that would help us: most companies ask for product a week or two before they actually needed it, and most customers can rearrange their schedule to some degree. I told our sales people to call every customer and find out when they absolutely had to have each order completed. I told them how many dollars of production the plant could give them a day and no more. In just a few days, basic as it was, we had a schedule. We worked hard and in six weeks, the plant was doing what it was supposed to do. Meanwhile, I had worked with my folks to come up with a better system based on man-hours. Employee morale went up. The president of the company thought I was a genius. I certainly was not; it was as my college advisor had said, most things are basic.

That was the start of a successful career later interrupted three times by job loss. All would be going well at work and I would start having nightmares; that led to loss of sleep. Indeed, I was almost afraid to fall asleep. This lack of sleep led to an inability to function in the daytime. I would go to my family doctor; he would treat me for depression. That rarely helped.

My nightmares tended to fall into categories. The first category was the terribly frightening dreams. I would wake my wife flailing, sometimes screaming, frightened, horrified. She would shake me awake. I would have been in some sort of inescapable situation. Yet, other than in the most general of terms, I would remember the terrifying dreams only briefly if at all. The second category was dreams of victorious historical fiction. I would be in my jungle fatigues, have my machine gun, be with the few backers of Cleopatra, and ambush Caesar on the boat dock just as he landed in Egypt. I would be in South Carolina during our Revolution and ambush the savage Colonel Tarleton as he led his troops out of their garrison. I would be at the Stone Bridge at Antietam or take out Al Capone. I have wondered, why the two kinds of dreams? I think that the horrible dreams were due to combat and the historical dreams were due to the loss of the war. My victorious dreams were seeking comfort.

Here are some examples of performance followed by job loss. I went to work as vice president of manufacturing at a company in the piedmont of Virginia. The company had three plants. We were very profitable and had the best employee benefits of any company of its kind in the area. Soon, the company president promoted me to vice president of operations and gave me a seat on the board of directors. Being profitable, we had two larger companies try to buy us. Finally, a company succeeded. They made me general manager and life went on. I went back to graduate school at night, had a number of my articles published in trade magazines, had a monthly column in one, and spoke many times to trade organizations. Indeed, after fifteen years with the company, life became easy.

That is when the nightmares started. That is when I went to my family doctors several times. I began just sitting in my office staring at the walls. I was in pain. My boss and I parted ways.

From there I went to work for my alma mater teaching in industry. I was busy with a new and challenging job where I learned a great deal, for a part of my job was visiting manufacturing facilities and helping companies solve their problems. One of the organizations I helped was impressed and hired me as president of one of their companies. That led to other opportunities but the nightmares had become a regular visitor costing me another job.

Finally, I went to my last job in industry. There I had some initial successes, but horrible dreams became a nasty, nightly occurrence. With little sleep, I was almost non-functional. I visited a young doctor who had just opened his practice. He had done a part of his residence at a Veterans Administration (VA) hospital. He recognized my symptoms. He said, "You have Post Traumatic Stress Disorder (PTSD). You need to go to the VA immediately."

My Veterans of Foreign Wars post advised me to see our Rep for Vets, an office set by our state to help vets like me get into the VA medical system. He carefully listened to me asking a number of questions. He felt like I needed to immediately see a VA doctor and receive total disability. That led to an appointment with a VA psychiatrist.

Our first meeting was via teleconference. He recognized my weariness, my hyper-alertness and that I was emotionally exhausted. He said that I had PTSD. However, I was afraid to admit how sick I was. I tried to be macho and say I knew I could overcome this. I am now of the opinion that, if this interview had been in person rather than on teleconference, he would have immediately slapped me in the hospital. He asked me whether I wanted help or just compensation. I said I wanted to get well.

The psychiatrist put me on six medicines; the prescriptions were at my door in two days. Soon after starting the medications, not only did I sleep at night, I took forty winks in a restaurant, my face in roast beef and potatoes. I was not embarrassed – I just did not care – sleep was great. My wife called my psychiatrist and he adjusted the dose of one medicine. The VA moved fast. The entire process from visiting that young doctor to being in this video conference to having my face in potatoes took little time.

The psychiatrist said that it had taken forty years to get into this sad shape, and it was going to take years to dig out of this pit. I went to inform my boss. I respected him greatly. His management style emulated George Patton's. That management style enabled his company to survive in a rapidly changing business climate. However, Patton did not believe in combat fatigue; neither did my boss. He acted as if he did not hear what I was telling him. While sleep was now easy, the side effects of the drugs were loss of my short-term memory. I often could not remember a report I had read only minutes before. That was extremely frustrating for me and I tried my boss's patience. After a few years, and numerous butt chewings, I was finally fired.

Meanwhile, I was meeting my psychiatrist via teleconference every day. That became weekly and finally monthly. My psychiatrist's approach was to help me to accept that combat happened then and this is now. After a year or two, the VA opened a new facility and I had a new psychiatrist. While his fundamental approach was the same, this psychiatrist was more of a listener. He exposed me to an arsenal of tools, things I could do that did not involve medications. Indeed, using those tools, I was able to get off one medication and then the next.

While my doctor introduced me to a number of things that helped, four stand out as being most effective. The first one that my psychiatrist taught me was avoidance of triggers. PTSD triggers are those things that activate war memories. For example, Vietnam War movies – I do not watch them. Jane Fonda television appearances and movies – I do not watch them. Indeed, if I am in a theater and something about Vietnam or Jane Fonda appears unexpectedly, I get up and leave immediately. Another example: television news usually has a piece on some war – I do not watch it. I am to the point that I watch our local channels' weather forecasts and only very carefully watch or read national news. In general, any kind of violence upsets me.

Other triggers such as pictures of children and displaced civilians in a war zone sadden me. Seeing combat-injured GIs hurts me. I walk a great deal on a local State Park's trails. Seeing a stranger approach puts me on alert causing me to watch his or her every move. When getting close, I smile and say, "Hello," and they usually return a pleasant response making me more relaxed, but I am never at ease until I have seen them on the trail many times.

I cannot watch adult theme movies; if it is not a G or PG-rated movie produced by Disney, I am likely not to be interested. Indeed, my grandchildren sometimes phone and say, "Paw Paw, I saw a movie you can watch. It is about ...." I often fear that my wife or some member of my family is going to get in a car and I will never see them again. All of these things used to cause strong emotions. To a lesser degree they still do; however, the VA has helped me form protective habits.

Part of avoiding triggers is avoiding troubling situations. When I do go to a restaurant or theater, I like to sit where I can see all of the people there. Further, I quickly spot all of the exits just in case something should happen. Anywhere that I feel trapped, I am uncomfortable. Both my psychiatrist and my social worker have said that I am the very kind of person that they would want to be with should they find themselves in a dangerous situation. Why? I would immediately revert to my combat mind, identify the possible enemy, and take some logical action.

The second thing the VA psychiatrist did was introduce me to my VA social worker. She had me remember one frightening combat incident at a time and analyze it in an orderly, structured manner. We then reviewed the incident together. We must have gone through a dozen such incidents. That process was painful at first, remembering combat events is simply upsetting. However, I soon learned that remembering, analyzing, and writing the events down took them out of the present and put them into the past where they belong. Past events become history. That process eventually led to writing this book.

The third helpful process the VA sent me through was going to a VA doctor who specialized in sleep. Yes, there are sleep doctors. He, too, gave me ways of relaxing, overcoming years of fearing sleep. I am still weak in this area and often have to take sleep medication. After a night or two of "bad dreams," I use sleeping pills for four or five nights to stop a nightmare pattern from reforming.

The fourth thing that helped was yoga. This process was not in the VA quiver, but my psychiatrist did find me a book (*Yoga for Warriors*, by Beryl Birch) and a well-qualified instructor whose rates I could afford. I thought yoga was some kind of weird kind of exercising. That is not what the instructor emphasized. Yes, she taught me certain yoga positions, but her emphasis was on "being in the present." When she had me assume a yoga position, she had me be aware of the air going in and out of my lungs. She had me concentrate on how my feet, leg muscles, knees, and on up to the top of my head felt, focusing on one muscle and then the next in a slow, purposeful way. While this practice is relaxing, it is much more about being aware of myself right now. It took me away from whatever was on my mind and put me "in the present." PTSD is living in the past. This is now. Next to visiting with my psychiatrist, writing about my combat events, and yoga were the most helpful process I have learned.

The only help I was not interested in was a kind of group therapy. In this process, a group of vets gets together and, one at the time, each relates something from his or her past. I wanted no part of that. Too often, I have heard a few vets get together and while one relates his story, some other old soldier's ego has to have a more frightening story to tell. Soon, you find yourself in the room with a John Wayne wannabe. I had and have no interest in that.

After more than a decade with the VA, I am off five of the medications and just use sleeping pills and those not all of the time. One of the primary reasons for writing this book is finally to rid myself of even the sleeping pills. My Christianity has paid a large role in my recovery and led to a new career as a pastor. I have accepted that combat and its residual, PTSD, will never completely depart from me. My wife's loving duty will long be to wake me from another nightmare. However, thanks to the Veterans Administration's help and my work as a Methodist pastor, I have learned to manage the worst of my problems, to put most of my memories in the past where they belong. I have shared some of my war experiences, told you some of the VA treatments that have helped, and told you that I am better; may my recollections help you understand that there is more than hope for those who suffer with Post Traumatic Stress Disorder.

In summary, I had successful jobs where I worked hard, long hours and had a wonderful family only to go through periods of nightmares and sparse sleep resulting in job losses, job changes. Civilian doctors did not understand; they treated me with antidepressants, temporary fixes if that. I found help at the Veterans Administration. Unfortunately, some of the early medicines the VA had to put me on to calm me down affected my short-term memory. That cost me a job and ultimately ended my business career. Today, I am happy. I am enjoying working again. Like other old soldiers, I wonder what I could have accomplished had I not had been plagued with war memories.

One final remark; I left college and joined the army because my country was at war. I wanted to fight. I did. It was nothing glorious like a jet fighter pilot or a Navy Seal, and I did not wear a Green Beret. I was just plain light infantry. I learned to hate war. I hate nightmares. PTSD is no fun. However, if called upon, I would not hesitate to do it again. I will always be part soldier.

Chapter 19: Do You Need the Help of a Healthcare Professional?

What is PTSD? The National Institute of Mental health defined it this way: "PTSD is a disorder in some people who have experienced a shocking, scary, or dangerous event." That does not tell you much. How do you know if you are one of "some people"? You would be a rare human being if you have not experienced "a shocking, scary, or dangerous event." How do you know when you have PTSD? I will explain what happens and give you some examples.

Feeling stress in our fast-paced, modern lives is as normal as sleeping. Experiencing something traumatic, something that is appalling, terrifying, maybe even dangerous hopefully happens far less often, but it is still something we all experience. When confronted with possible danger your nervous system responds in a split second. This response can happen in the face of a rather ordinary event such as having to make a speech at school to something as frightening as running across an aggressive, teeth-bared, growling dog to a very serious event like facing an armed robber. Your adrenal glands release adrenaline and other hormones that result in an increase in your heart rate, blood pressure, and breathing rate. From the ordinary to the severe situations, real or perceived, your body prepares to perform under pressure, to either struggle through the situation or flee. This is called the fight-or-flight response. Your body's fight-or-flight response makes it more likely that you will cope effectively with the threat.

Irrational fears are good examples of how perceived threats trigger the fight-or-flight response. One evening, you begin to experience an acute stress response when you have to go to the top floor of a tall hotel for a night's stay. You look out the window of your high hotel room and down at the street hundreds of feet below; you feel the wind sway the building just a bit. That does it. You are scared. Your body goes on high alert increasing your heartbeat and respiration rate. The response becomes severe; it leads to a *panic attack*. You start looking for ways to calm down and relax your body. You decide on flight; you get another room on the ground floor. The threat is gone. It still takes between twenty and sixty minutes for all of your body's reactions to return to normal.

For you that may be the end of it; you would likely forget that event in a day or three. However, you may have been scared enough to say, "I'll never go high in a tall building again." Or, worse, this simple event may have been extremely frightening for you. It may cause nightmares and, with them, your body again goes on high alert. You are now terrified of heights. This may seem irrational to you, the reader, but it happens.

What else might cause this kind of fear? Pick one: being raped, robbed with a knife at your throat, being molested as a child, being in a terrifying wreck spattered with blood and brains, falling into a well at three years old and not being rescued for seventeen hours, seeing a family member beaten, hiding in a closet on Christmas while your drunken family fought, or mortal combat.

The variables are as numerous as the causes: How often did it happen? For a store owner to be robbed once is bad, being robbed twelve times as has happened to one store owner in the Bronx is worse. How intense was or were the experiences? Half a dozen hoodlums rob you, kicking you repeatedly, your body automatically balling into the fetal position, the thugs screaming, "Kill him!" as they conquer you. You are unconscious. Had the police not shown up, you would be dead. Your experience was beyond intense. You spent months in the hospital recovering. As in any traumatic event, your mind had to decide to run or fight but you could not run; you could not fight. The thugs had you for their pleasure.

You lived through the event but you were so horrified that your mind began to dredge up the event again and again. You relived the suffering past the point of desperation. There is no stopping it. The memories are every bit as horrible as the event they remember. Your return to some pre-arousal level takes longer and longer every time you relive the experience. Even related events trigger the memory. With even minor perceived treats, you become hyper-alert. You have PTSD. If you are lucky, you may learn to live with a bad memory in weeks, maybe even months, but maybe not.

In chronic cases, whether a singular event such as a rape, or with multiple memories as often occurs in combat, your mind, body, and spirit establish a new normal; fight-or-flight arousal becomes permanent, a steady state. You may become distant from others, avoiding anything that reminds you of the event or events. You will not discuss your fears with even those to whom you are close. You may become jumpy, constantly on guard. You may well become irritable, having outbursts of anger. There may be flashbacks. Nightmares may become so common that you fear even falling asleep. There is no rest. You may be so exhausted that you cannot work effectively, for you are in pain, confused; job loss is next. You may have the fear that you, or those you love, will die early.

Your fears and nightmares are constantly present; they become burned into your mind and, inevitably into that most authentic part of your personality, your very soul. PTSD results in a reorganization of everything about you, how your body works, how you see things; even your spirit is hard hit. That means that any cure has to affect how you view your memories, the mental, physical, and spiritual changes your body has made in trying to deal with the problem, the ongoing crisis in that part of you that makes you who you are has changed.

You must lay aside the idea that you can whip this on your own and be willing to accept guidance. It took me years, even after I had found help, to accept that I was not a super strong macho man. I wanted to believe that I was better than I was. I told my psychiatrist that I was better than I was. It took professional help and my wife's criticism finally to succumb and admit to myself that I was sick.

Your objective is not to escape your memory or memories but to learn to live a happy, productive life. You do this by admitting that you have PTSD. Your memories are a permanent part of you, but they are in the past and this is now. The trick is to make your past into what it is, a part of your personal *history*. It is over. It will take time and work to overcome the damage that reliving that memory or memories over and over caused. If the cause happened forty years ago, you have had forty years of repeated exposure to the terror, for your mind does not know the difference between the event and your reliving it. There is no pill you can take; there is no magic dust that a witch doctor can sprinkle you with to fix it. Yet, the rewards, the freedom, make the time and the hard work that you must invest to move on with your life, well worth every ounce of effort.

Chapter 20: An Important Part of Healing:
Forgiveness

As you have read, my first combat was only a few days after I arrived in Vietnam. On one my first nights in combat, the man to my immediate right, whose shoulder was only a foot away from my own, got a nose full of grenade shrapnel. The invincibility of my youth left me swiftly. I knew that I could die. I wrote each letter home with care, for I suddenly knew that each letter might be the last words my loved ones would ever read from me.

Since realizing that, I have noted the last words of a number of famous people. I have found that a person's dying words can be revealing, showing us something of the person. The ideas of Karl Marx put many nations on the horrible road to communism. On the day Marx died, March 14, 1883, his housekeeper came to him and said, "Mr. Marx, tell me your last words, and I'll write them down." Marx replied, "Go, get out! Last words are for fools who haven't said enough!" P.T. Barnum, the founder of the Barnum and Bailey Greatest Show on Earth, asked as he was dying, "What are the receipts of the day?" Napoleon's last words were, "I am Chief of the Army!" The great Baptist preacher Charles Spurgeon's last words were, "Jesus died for me." And Charles Wesley, the initiator of the Methodist Church, said, "Best of all is, God is with us."

The Bible records seven last statements that Christ uttered while he was on the cross. These

statements are important to us, not only because
Jesus spoke them, but also because of the place
where he said them. While Christ was on the cross,
he was doing his greatest work; he was uttering
some of his greatest words. Luke 23:34 records one
of his last statements: "Then Jesus said, 'Father,
forgive them, for they do not know what they do.'"
Sometimes it is difficult for us to forgive people.
Sometimes it is difficult for us to forgive ourselves.
Someone hurts us, someone says something against
us, and in our hearts, we cannot forgive that person.
Or maybe we hurt someone.

Listen to Jesus' prayer: "Father, forgive them,
for they do not know what they do." Jesus prayed
these words of forgiveness on behalf of the people
gathered at the foot of the cross; people who wanted
to watch him die; people who only the day before
had shouted, "Crucify Him!" Jesus spoke these
words of forgiveness on behalf of the Roman
soldiers, the people who only minutes before had
nailed him to the cross. He said it for the members
of the Sanhedrin who had rushed to find him guilty
of a capital crime. He said it for his frightened
disciples who had run and were in hiding. Notice
the wonder of his words. Understanding his final
example to us will enable us to forgive others, to
forgive ourselves, and to experience the joy that
comes when we do forgive. We need to know that
God forgives us for our sins.

Christ had a world-changing attitude. I hear
Christians say, "I cannot talk to God! I cannot pray!
I do not believe anymore – after the way people

have treated me." Look at the way people treated Jesus. He had preached love. He had healed the sick. He had fed the poor. He had done nothing bad to anyone. His only crime was to upset the social order. For this, his nation sinned against him. His own disciples failed him. Peter denied him. His heavenly Father was willing to see him suffer. He was up all night, dragged from one kangaroo court to another, found guilty of crimes he did not commit, beaten almost beyond recognition, had multiple stab wounds in the head from the thorns in his crown, made to drag his own cross, pierced with spikes driven through his hands and feet, then raised on the cross, suspended by his nail-torn flesh between two thieves to suffer death.

In spite of all this, Jesus was able to look up into the heavens and begin his prayer with, "Father." He lived in fellowship with his Father and knew that even under these horrible circumstances, God loved him. I remember in Matthew chapter 22, verses 34 through 37, the Pharisees asked Jesus, " 'Teacher, which is the great commandment in the law?' and Jesus answered, 'You shall love the Lord your God with all your heart, with all your soul, and with all your mind.'" Jesus, under these most difficult circumstances of his life, remained true to his Father, never doubting God's love, even while nailed to the cross.

Perhaps you are hurting now. You are thinking, "If God loves me, how can he let me suffer so?" God loved Jesus, and yet he was willing to see Jesus die a horrible death. No matter how bad things seem, God loves us, and he always will; have no doubt in that. Do not lose faith. He is working out his purpose for each of us. Christ's agony on that cross was for the greatest purpose. God raised him to eternal glory. It is not easy to suffer. Pain hurts. It seems so unfair. A broken heart hurts far worse than a broken arm. If we really want to be a Christian, Jesus, here on the cross, shows us where we must start. We must start by following God's will, no matter if our circumstances seem as dark as those that Jesus faced on the cross that day more than two thousand years ago. When we can say, "Father," then we are able to look up to heaven and know that God will make all right.

Next in Christ's appeal, we find "forgive them." "Father, forgive them." The Greek New Testament indicates that our Lord repeated this prayer several times. He said it as they laid him on the cross as it lay on the ground. He said it as they drove the spikes through his flesh. He said it as they raised his cross, its base sliding into a hole in the ground, jerking erect with a sudden and painful thud. And finally, he said it as he hung there, dangled in the air by his mangled meat. "Father, forgive them." He could have prayed, "Father, judge them; Father, bring punishment upon them." He could have called down legions of angels to deliver him, but he did not. The thing that kept Christ on that cross was love, not nails. I say again, the thing that kept Christ on that cross was love, not nails. Jesus knew what was going to happen to him.

He knew he was going to the cross. He could have run.

Luke 22:21 records what Jesus said the night before he was betrayed, at the Last Supper, "But behold, the hand of My betrayer is with Me on the table." Christ told Judas to go do what he had to do. Jesus could have slipped out of that room and out of Jerusalem as soon as Judas was gone. He did not. A short time later, Jesus went to the Garden of Gethsemane to pray before Judas showed up with the temple guards. Jesus could have run then. I read portions from Luke 22:39-46, "Coming out, He went to the Mount of Olives, as He was accustomed, and His disciples also followed Him. When He came to the place … He was withdrawn from them about a stone's throw, and He knelt down and prayed, saying, 'Father, if it is Your will, take this cup away from Me; nevertheless not My will, but Yours, be done.' … And being in agony, He prayed more earnestly. Then His sweat became like great drops of blood falling down to the ground." Jesus knew what was coming. He had the power to turn and walk away from the horrible pain that he knew the Romans would inflict on him, and yet he said, "not My will, but Yours [Father], be done." Jesus went to the cross because he loved us. He went to the cross knowing he would pray, "Father, forgive them."

Many times some of us may have wanted to bring down fire from heaven on someone and wanted to pray, "Father, judge them for their sin against me." But our Lord gave us his example that day: "Father, forgive them." Christ practiced the message that he preached. He preached forgiveness. He told his people in his messages, "Now, if you do not forgive from your heart, God cannot forgive you." This does not mean that the basis of forgiveness is our own good works. No, but it does mean that if in our hearts we are unwilling to forgive others, we are in no condition to come and ask God for forgiveness for ourselves. Let me repeat that: If we are unwilling to forgive others, we are in no shape to enter into God's presence and ask for forgiveness. Forgiveness of a wrong against us is a form of mastering ourselves, of moving to Christ-likeness. We must remember that all of this happened while Rome ruled the world. The Romans worshipped revenge. Revenge was one of their gods. Revenge is the god of the terrorists that flew airplanes full of innocent people into the Twin Towers, murdering 3,000 innocent souls whom God created in his image. Our Lord Jesus did not worship revenge, nor should we. He prayed, "Father, forgive them," and in doing so, he fulfilled the Word. He practiced his own message of forgiveness.

This, of course, was the purpose of his death. Our Lord was on the cross because God does forgive sinners. That is the message of the Gospels. We do not have to go around with the weight and burden of anger and revenge on our lives. We do not have to carry the guilt of sin. We can forgive! We can be forgiven! Forgiveness is the message of the cross. Forgiveness is not cheap; it is very expensive. It cost Jesus his life. We will have no problem forgiving others if we are right in our relationship with our Father and remember that <u>God has forgiven us</u>. Those who do not forgive others tear down the bridge on which they themselves will have to walk. Romans chapter 3, verse 23 states, "for all have sinned and fall short of the glory of God." God loves us. We are rebellious, we act selfishly, we are immoral, we sin, yet God loves us intensely. He loves us beyond anything that we can comprehend. He loves us so much that he gave his only son, Jesus the Christ, to die on that cross.

Perhaps some will argue, "But you have no idea how others have treated me." Well, I have an idea of how others treated Jesus, and yet he was able to say, "Father, forgive them, for they do not know what they do." Our Lord not only prayed for the forgiveness of his enemies, but with this last phrase, he argued on their behalf and your behalf. It is as though he stood as a lawyer and said to his Father, "Let me give you a reason why you should forgive them. They do not know what they do. They are ignorant of the enormity of their actions. They do not realize what great sinners they are. I know what I am doing; I am dying for them. Now, Father, forgive them so that I will not have died in vain, that I may, in this most horrible of circumstances, set a final example."

The early New Testament Scriptures, written mostly in Greek, commonly used the word *aphesis* to convey the English "forgiveness." *Aphesis* means "sending away" or "letting go." Quite simply put,

"Father, forgive them, for they do not know what they do" is letting go. It is the understanding of the basic fact that good is permanent, always present, and all-powerful. Evil is temporary, insubstantial, and without its own character. The trick is the proper spiritual treatment of evil. Do not wrestle with evil. Forgive yourself and forgive others. Not to forgive a wrong done to us or by us is to give further life and power to that evil. Not to forgive is to transfer power onto our memories and any person who has hurt us. This makes matters worse. How foolish. Evil cannot come into our lives unless there is something in us with which it is attuned. By forgiving that wrong, not only do we remove its ability to do us more harm, we remove the likelihood of retaliation, we present the wrongdoer with an example that may change him.

Paul covers this point quite well in Romans Chapter 12, verses 17-21, "Repay no one evil for evil. Have regard for good things in the sight of all men. If it is possible, as much as depends on you, live peaceably with all men. Beloved, do not avenge yourselves, but rather … 'If your enemy is hungry, feed him; If he is thirsty, give him a drink…' Do not be overcome by evil, but overcome evil with good." God loves us; he wants us to be happy.

While on the cross, Christ was still thinking only of your happiness and you. His final words about forgiving apply to any wrong you have done. His final words about forgiving even those who have horribly wronged you are a part of your guide to the happiness God wants for you. When you will not forgive yourself or someone else, you are expressing a degree of hate. That hate has negative psychological and physiological effects on you. Hatred is one of the most destructive emotions. Indeed, every time you think about something you did that was wrong or that someone did to you, you relive whatever reason you think you have for hating. You become the victim of your own thoughts. That is why you are not to bear a grudge or seek vengeance. I mean, even though someone has harmed you in some way, every time you remember that harm or seek vengeance or bear a grudge, you relive the pain. Your emotions do not allow you to differentiate between the real and the imagined. In your mind, you become victims again. Only by removing the hatred, through forgiveness, do you release the pain and remove the ability of your memories to keep hurting you again and again. Forgiveness means you no longer victimize yourself. This reliving of your victimhood is why God forbids you to seek vengeance. You shall not repay evil with evil. You are to return good for evil (Matthew 5:43-48). Jesus says that in so doing, maybe you will make an enemy into a friend. Only forgiveness removes your sin of hatred. By forgiving, you remove the ability of that wrong to do you more harm. Forgiveness is for your happiness; forgiveness is God's mercy on you, the victim of a horror or a wrong. Forgiveness breaks the cycle and lets you get on with your life. Forgiveness removes you from victim status.

"Father, forgive them, for they do not know what they do." Again, I say, nails did not hold Jesus on the cross, love did. Jesus' last words from the cross give you an example of how you may join Christ in his work on earth. These last words show you how to slip from evil's hold on your life. Jesus, while suffering to death on the cross, showed you another way to help establish his kingdom on earth.

You have a complete Bible, from Adam to Christ's second coming. You are not ignorant of the requirement that all Christians must forgive themselves and all who have sinned against you. You are not to carry revenge in your heart. It will hurt you much more than it will hurt the ones who have wronged you. God is patient with you, that you may have time to reconcile yourself with your sins, and he asks you to treat others the same way. Is that too much?

Religion is in rapid decline in America and the world. I believe that is because we Christians have too many high-sounding words, and too few actions. Jesus' instructions are simple: Forgive!

Love yourself. Love others as you love yourself. Forgiveness begins when you realize that God has forgiven you. Whatever sins you have committed, if you sincerely go to God and ask for forgiveness, they are forgiven. Then, if possible, ask for forgiveness from those against whom you sinned.

Now, search your heart. Are you trying to crucify yourself? Is there someone you hate so much that for you to meet them on the street is to suffer? Is there someone who has you in victim status? Is there someone you hate so much that you would not tell them about Christ? Is there someone whom you need to forgive? If there is, know that Christ wants you free of your pain: Forgive! Forgive that you may do what Christ would have you do. Forgive that you may enjoy life better. Forgive that you may join Christ in establishing his way as your way. Forgiveness puts you in a position to witness to all.